P9-CCH-254

How to Arrange Flowers
for All Occasions

(Photo by Roche)   *Arrangement by Catherine H. Smith*

How to Arrange Flowers
for All Occasions

Katherine N. Cutler

Doubleday & Company, Inc., Garden City, New York

To Westy,
whose constant help and encouragement has made
this book possible.

Linecut illustrations by Rebekah H. Collins

Library of Congress Catalog Card Number 67–12874
Copyright © 1967 by Katherine N. Cutler
Copyright © 1964 by Nelson Doubleday, Inc.
All Rights Reserved
Printed in the United States of America

CONTENTS

INTRODUCTION

THE ART of flower arranging is not new. From early paintings and tapestries there is evidence that flowers had an important place in the life of people everywhere. For centuries the Japanese especially have been known for their arrangements of classic beauty.

In this country, however, it is only in comparatively recent years that more and more people are discovering the stimulation, satisfaction, and relaxation of creating beautiful pictures with plant material instead of paint, clay, or stone. Already established as one of the fine arts, flower arranging is rapidly taking its place with cooking and sewing as an important creative household art. Some quality of charm is missing in a home that has no living plant material. The pioneer women of our country knew this when they took precious packets of flower seeds with them on their journeys West, and grew a few bright blossoms in utilitarian containers in the windows or around the doorsteps of their crude cabins. They didn't have time to arrange flowers, but they knew they could not get along without them as part of their daily life.

Flower arranging is an art, but it is an art that almost anyone can master. I don't mean that an enthusiastic novice will immediately win a blue ribbon in a flower show—although she might. I do mean that the woman who realizes that her home is incomplete without the beauty of flowers can open her eyes to the abundance of material that Nature has provided all around her, and with the aid of some helpful suggestions, find great joy through artistic expression, and just plain fun in making beautiful arrangements.

Some people have made an intensive study of design, color, and allied subjects and applied this to plant material. These are the ones who teach, lecture, write, and exhibit in large flower shows. This is very different from arranging flowers in a home for relaxation and pleasure. Making an exhibit for a flower show is hard, intensive, concentrated work. Exhibitors spend many hours on one exhibit, doing research, collecting material, and finally practicing until each detail is as perfect as possible, for· they know the arrangement will be judged by experts against perfection according to a scale of points. Invariably the night before a show they work late. Recently, one of my friends, whose husband was on a business trip in California, was working on her exhibit the night before an important show. At 3 A.M. the telephone rang. An operator said, "San Francisco calling," whereupon a male voice came on the wire saying, "Go to bed!"

I won't say that it isn't a great thrill to win a ribbon in a flower show—it is. But I don't think there is the pure pleasure that comes from bringing some flowers or leaves into your house and making an arrangement that really satisfies *you*. And wonderful as flower shows are, I think some of the advanced and, to the untutored eye, weird arrangements on exhibit have confused and frightened would-be arrangers.

One of my biggest thrills still is to see a florist approach my door with one of those long white boxes, and I am horrified at the number of women who take containers to a florist for him to fill, instead of having the fun of selecting and arranging the flowers themselves. When I question them they say, "Oh, I don't know anything about arranging flowers. When I hear Mrs. So and So who wins all those blue ribbons discussing rhythmic sequence, dominance of luminosity, and split complements, I don't even know what she is talking about!"

The fact that you may know someone who is more experienced and talks about flower arranging in technical terms should never intimidate you. There is plenty of time for further study. In the meantime, just pitch in and choose flowers that appeal to you and start arranging, and keep on arranging and arranging. The important thing is not to be timid about it, and to like what you do. When I first started exhibiting in shows, an experienced exhibitor gave me a piece of advice I have never forgotten. She said, "If you are proud to have your name on your exhibit, whether or not you win a ribbon is unimportant."

The same thing applies to arranging flowers in your own home. If it pleases you, how other people like your arrangement is unimportant—nice if they do, but still unimportant. Anyone who has had a great deal of training in arranging flowers has had the experience of going to a house and having the hostess say, "Oh, please don't look at my flowers," or "I was worried about my flower arrangements when I heard you were coming." Believe me, this is very irritating. The fact that a guest is more experienced in working at flower arranging should never make a hostess self-conscious. The so-called expert isn't going to be any more critical of her hostess's flowers than she is of her costume or of the cheese soufflé she is serving.

The next time you are out for a walk, look around you with a "seeing eye" and discover something you may not have noticed before that could be the nucleus of an interesting arrangement. It might be a beautifully curved pine branch, a gnarled root, early clusters of chartreuse Norway maple tree flowers (yes, many trees have blossoms), or some dried seed pods in a field. Once you get this habit, you will almost never come home empty-handed.

The fact that material for an arrangement does not have to be florist grown, highly cultivated, or expensive to be desirable was graphically illustrated to me one day when I watched two women working on exhibits side by side at the International Flower Show in New York. One woman was working with sprays of orchids, heedlessly letting the blossoms fall to the floor as she snipped to get the proper line. The second woman was doing a naturalistic arrangement with bare branches and skunk cabbage. When I returned after the judging, I found the naturalistic arrangement—a beautiful study in line—had won the blue ribbon, while the orchid arrangement received honorable mention.

Flower arranging is such a wonderful means of self-expression it can be a truly joyous experience, and should never be approached with trepidation or frustration. My aim in this book is to try and convey my great enthusiasm and share with you some of the pleasures and problems of many happy flower arranging years. My hope is that, inspired by the beauty in the world around you and helped by the knowledge of some fundamental principles of art and mechanical aids which we will discuss, you will create lovely arrangements.

But above all, I hope that you will have fun doing it.

I

General Flower Arrangement

PRINCIPLES OF DESIGN IN FLOWER ARRANGING

PEOPLE say, "How do you start making a flower arrangement? Do you choose the flowers first and then find a container to suit them? Do you have a vase you want to use and then find flowers to go with it? Or do you decide you want an arrangement for a certain place and then find a container and flowers for it?"

The answer is that there is no one set way to start. Any of the above methods will work. For instance, if you find a branch or a flower stalk that suggests a design, you would choose a container that is right for that design, and proceed from there. Or, if the florist arrives with a gift assortment of flowers or a neighbor brings you an armful from her garden, you would decide where in your house they would look best, according to their color and size, and then choose a container to fit the flowers and background. If there is a container that you want to use, you think of a design that would look well in it, and then get your plant material. For a dining table centerpiece, the size and shape of the table and the general decoration of the room would determine the flowers and container to use.

No matter how you start, there are a few rules of good design that can make the difference between your arrangement looking like a work of art, or just flowers haphazardly stuck in a vase. These principles don't apply only to flower arrangement. You use them in the way you place furniture in your rooms, and in the way you choose your clothes. You have used them so often that you probably will find that you are applying most of them instinctively. But a conscious knowledge of these rules, and how to apply them to flower arrangement, will give you confidence.

Most flower arrangements fall under three headings: line arrangements which the Japanese have done so exquisitely for centuries; mass arrangements, which are full bouquets, typical of Victorian, English eighteenth-century, French, and Flemish arrangements; and line mass arrangements—not so sparse as line or as abundant as mass. Examples of line arrangements are the miniature one in Plate 2 and the one of wisteria vine in Fig. 19. Mass arrangements are the arrangement of foliage and flowers in Fig. 10 and the garden flowers in Plate 8. Line mass arrangements are the one of roses in Plate 7, the dried material in Plate 12, and the tropical one in Fig. 1.

Arrangement by Katherine N. Cutler

Figure 1. A colorful line mass arrangement of tropical material using jade-green casuarina cones, flame-colored bayonet tree, and firecracker bush, and yellow gerbera and croton. (Photo by Thomas W. Hall, Bermuda)

Pattern

Whether it is line or mass, each arrangement should have a *pattern* or *design*. It may be triangular, oval, rectangular, crescent, fan, or any other established shape. The Hogarth line, sometimes called the reverse curve, or the S curve, is one of the most beautiful. Sometimes the shape of an arrangement is suggested by the plant material—a curving piece of wisteria vine might suggest a crescent, or some stalks of snapdragon a triangle. Sometimes a container seems to call for a particular shape and you select plant material accordingly.

Everyone develops his own way of proceeding to make an arrangement, but this is the way I find that I invariably do it. After I have the flowers and container, I plan what mechanical aids I will need to hold the flowers where I want them for the design I have in mind, and fasten them in place. Then I establish the main lines of the arrangement—make a skeleton, in other words. If it is to be a triangle, for instance, I put in the line for height, and the two side pieces. If it is to be circular or crescent-shaped, I put in the main curves. Then I put in some material at the focal point.

Each flower arrangement must have a *focal point,* which is just *Focal Point* what the name implies—a center of interest at the point where all the lines of the arrangement come together. If you picture an imaginary line drawn from the top of the arrangement to the bottom of the container, and another line drawn from one side to the other at its widest point, the spot at which these lines cross should be the focal point. A focal point gives stability to an arrangement and pulls it together. It is the spot where your eye comes to rest. It is here that you should put larger flower forms, and those of the darkest color.

I heard the child who made the Valentine arrangement in Fig. 33 explain this very well, when I overheard her say to the photographer who took the picture, "I call the lines of my arrangement the roads leading to the castle, and the center [focal point] the castle." If an arrangement is all "roads" and has no "castle," your eye keeps wandering around and around, looking for a place to rest.

When I have made the outline or skeleton of an arrangement, and established the focal point, I fill in with other flowers, following the general outline, and using different flower forms for interest. I turn some of the flowers so that they are in profile. This is more interesting, and gives depth and dimension to the arrangement. An arrangement of daffodils, for instance, with all the trumpets facing forward would be flat and uninteresting.

I am careful to leave some spaces between the flowers around the outside edge. These are called *voids* and are very desirable. They give the arrangement a spacious feeling, and keep it from looking crowded and heavy. On the other hand, spaces in the middle of an arrangement are merely holes, and are not desirable. They weaken the design.

As a finishing touch, I tuck some of the flowers in the back of the arrangement for a dimensional look.

There are other qualities that a good flower arrangement has. None of them is difficult to achieve, once you become aware of them.

Proportion

There was a time when flower arrangers were thought to have a tape measure as part of their equipment. Thank goodness, those days of linear limits are past. While a flower container is a definite

In this drawing the arrangement is a triangular design. It has interesting voids and the proportion is good—higher than one and one-half times height of container, because of heavy base. Tip of top branch is over the center. Focal point of leaves and large flower is at point where line drawn from top to bottom meets line at widest part. Lighter flower forms are at perimeter of arrangement.

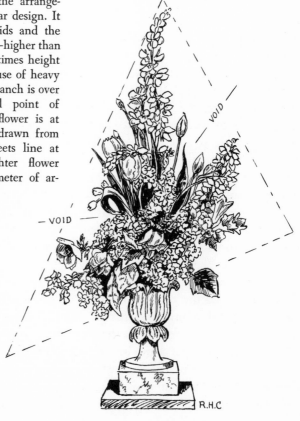

part of the flower arrangement as a whole, it should always be subordinate to the flowers in importance. Therefore the plant material should be enough taller than a tall vase, and enough wider than a low one, so that there is no doubt which is the more important of the two. In general, you are safe if your flowers are once and a half to twice the height of a tall container, or once and a half to twice the width of a low one. This is only a guide, however. An arrangement can be extremely tall if there is enough visual weight at the base.

It is extremely disconcerting to see an arrangement that looks *Balance* as though it might tip over at any minute. This happens when it is not balanced. Visual weight is very important in flower arranging, and is very simple to understand. I remember once giving a talk on flower arranging to some kindergartners before a school flower show. I held up two tulips of identical size, one white and one red, and asked which was the heavier. There was a chorus of "the red one." I explained that it only *looked* heavier, and that they both actually weighed the same.

Then I said, "Since the red tulip looks heavier, let's pretend it's a boy in the sixth grade, and the white one a boy from your class. If they are on a seesaw, where will the red tulip boy have to sit to make it balance?" Again there was a chorus, of "Near the middle." I explained then that for a flower arrangement to be balanced, the larger, darker flowers should be "near the middle." The children got the point so well that on the day of the show there was a big red flower in the middle of almost every kindergartner's arrangement.

Sometimes it happens that in the material you are using the darkest color is in the smallest flowers, like violets or purple sweet peas. You might say to yourself, "What do I do now? They say smaller flowers belong on the outside edges of an arrangement, but dark-colored ones should be near the center. How can these be both places?" The solution is to fasten the small flowers into a small bunch with tape or wire, and use them as you would one dark flower—near the center.

There should be proper *scale* or relation in size between the *Scale* flowers and the container. Most people have an intuitive sense about this. An adult sitting in a small child's chair would offend your intuitive sense of scale. So, I am sure would flowers whose forms are too large for a container. Four large daffodils would look ridiculous in a five-inch bud vase. So too, flowers should be in proper scale relationship to each other. Sweetheart roses, for instance, would be lost combined with large sprays of lilacs, but hybrid tea roses would be lovely.

Rhythm

A flower arrangement should have rhythm. This is accomplished by repetition of form or color which make the lines of the arrangement flow into each other. Solid forms decrease in size from the focal point, and voids increase.

Suitability

People also have an intuitive sense about the *suitability* of flowers and container. Just as most women wouldn't wear sneakers with a satin dress, so they wouldn't arrange hothouse orchids in an earthen pie plate. There should be a relationship between the flowers themselves, and the flowers and container in quality and texture.

Color

Color contributes to the design of an arrangement in the way it balances light and dark shades, but it does more than that. Color communicates. An arrangement in shades of green gives a feeling of serenity. A brilliant orange and flame combination excites you. A blending of soft colors—pink, rose, and violet can make you feel contented and that "all's right with the world." Some drab combinations are depressing, and a violent clash of color can make you almost physically sick.

Unless you want to be deliberately dramatic with contrast, handle colors so that they blend and there is a transition from one to the other. For instance, if you are making an arrangement in shades of yellow, blue, and lavender, and are using yellow acacia, at the top and sides of the arrangement, purple anemones at the focal point, and daffodils and blue iris in the rest, see that some anemone buds showing color, or dark iris buds, carry the purple color to the top of the arrangement, blending with the blue iris on its way up.

This transition of color is illustrated in the arrangement in Plate 8. The darker colors blend into each other. Most of the white flowers are properly at the outside edges, but the white color line is carried through the arrangement from the nicotiana at the lower right corner, through the white zinnias in the center, to the nicotiana and feverfew at the top left.

It is exciting, when assembling an arrangement, to find unexpected color accents—to see, for instance, how the dark red underside of a begonia leaf will bring out a pink highlight in a bronze container, or how you notice that some of the petals of a green hydrangea are really blue when placed next to a spray of gray-blue juniper berries.

The choice of color in a flower arrangement is a very personal thing. There are certain colors you prefer to others. You probably use them in your clothes and in the decoration of your house. You will probably use them in your flower arrangements. Remember, though, the place in which your arrangement will be. Don't get carried away doing one in shades of pinks to red and suddenly realize it's to be placed against a yellow wall next to orange curtains.

You can use color in your flower arrangement to emphasize another color in your room. I realized this one day in the fall when I went out in the yard to see what I could find to make an arrangement for the living room. It was to go on a table against a celadon green wall. There were no flowers, but plenty of foliage, so I gathered laurel, deep green ilex, and chartreuse andromeda, and for the focal point, dogwood leaves that were a gorgeous deep vibrant red. When I put the arrangement on the table, suddenly the same red sprang at me from various places in the room—a subordinate color note in the draperies, some tiny flowers in a needlepoint chair, some books in the bookshelves, and a red enameled ashtray on the coffee table. The dogwood leaves drew them all together.

Texture

There should be a strong relationship of texture in flowers and container. When you look at them you sense a tactile quality. You don't have actually to touch a pansy to know that it feels smooth and velvety. Looking at a pewter container with a smooth patina gives you much the same feeling. Therefore pansies arranged in a pewter porringer would be a happy combination.

A zinnia or a strawflower has a rough look, as does weathered wood, wicker, or driftwood. There would be a kinship here.

This does not mean that you must use only flowers and containers of the same textural feeling. Often the introduction of a contrast makes the arrangement more interesting. It does mean though that you should be aware of textural qualities and use them to the best advantage.

When you have completed an arrangement, you can give yourself a little test. Ask:

Is there a definite pattern in the arrangement?
Does it have a dimensional look?
Is there a center of interest or focal point?
Are the flowers and container suitable to each other in quality?
Is the color harmonious?
Are the flowers related in size and scale?
Is the arrangement balanced?
Are the flowers high or wide enough for the size of the container?
Are the flowers related to the container in size and scale?
Is there rhythm in the arrangement?
Have I been conscious of textural qualities?
Do I like this arrangement?
Have I enjoyed making it?

If you can answer yes to the first eleven questions, you can be confident that you have made a good arrangement and that it will please others too. But more important, if you can answer yes to the last two questions, you have found a hobby that will bring you inspiration and joy for the rest of your life.

SELECTING AND CONDITIONING
PLANT MATERIAL

MANY times the inspiration for an arrangement comes from seeing an unusual branch, some curling vine tendrils, or the buds or seed pods of a flower. It is amazing how, when your eye becomes trained to look for such things, you can't walk through the garden, in the woods, or along the roadside without seeing things you would have passed without noticing before. If you find a branch that intrigues you, visualize it in an arrangement, and then look for other branches that curve in the direction you need. Often you can find one that with just a little pruning is exactly right. Try to train yourself to see the skeletal line without being confused by leaves and side branches. These can be trimmed away, leaving a striking main line.

In choosing flowers for an arrangement, try and combine different shapes. An arrangement using just one shape is monotonous. There are round forms like daisies, carnations, or zinnias, tall spiky forms like delphiniums or stock, pendulant ones like fuchsia or wisteria, and those like daffodils or columbine, whose irregular form gives interest to a combination of other shapes.

There are the same forms in leaves. Geranium and galax leaves are round, iris and sansevieria are spiky, tradescantia and philodendron are pendulant, and rex begonia and ivy are irregular. When you are making an arrangement, if you want a certain form, and don't have it in flowers, you can substitute foliage in the same form.

If you buy flowers at a florist's, try and get a few buds. Some flowers like spray chrysanthemums, pinks, and marguerites have them anyway, but buying a few carnation or daffodil buds will be well worth the extra cost in adding interest to an arrangement.

It is very important to know how to condition flowers and foliage so that they will last as long as possible. When you cut a flower or a piece of foliage, it is deprived of its natural source of moisture. The length of time it will live depends on how quickly and fully its stem can be filled with water.

Cut flowers in the early morning or late afternoon if possible, so that the hot midday sun won't wilt them. Make a slanting cut with sharp shears so that there will be more surface of the stem to absorb water. It is a good idea to carry a container of water with you as you gather flowers so that they can be put in water immediately. You can make a convenient flower carrier for this purpose from fruit juice cans. Take three different-sized ones to a tinsmith and have him solder them together with a ring on the top for a handle. If you have this with you as you cut flowers, you can put them in the cans according to size.

As soon as possible put the flowers in water deep enough to cover three quarters of the stem, first stripping off any leaves or buds that won't add to the arrangement. Foliage that will be submerged, especially that on roses, chrysanthemums, and marigolds, will decay and foul the water and weaken the stems. To strip rose stems, hold them in your left hand and strip off leaves and thorns with a wad of newspaper. Breaking the thorns from rose stems opens more water absorbing areas. Leave the flowers in deep water for several hours, or preferably overnight.

It is a good idea too to recut the stems of florists' flowers, and give them a good soaking before you arrange them.

Some plant material requires special treatment before it is put in water to soak or, as we say, harden. The reasons for this are logical. Some flowers have a milky juice in the stems. If this juice drips away, the cells collapse and the flowers will droop. To prevent the juice escaping, sear the end of the cut immediately. You might take a candle and some matches with you for this purpose—a cigarette lighter would even be better. Flowers that need this treatment are milkweed, dahlias, pokeweed, poinsettias, mignonette, heliotrope, poppies, hollyhocks, and morning glories.

Flowers and shrubs with woody stems should have the ends of the stems slit up an inch or so, so that there will be more surface to absorb water. Some of these are chrysanthemums, stock, roses, and syringa.

In the case of shrubs with very heavy stems like lilacs, it helps to crush the ends of the stems with a heavy object, as shown in Fig. 2. It may be well to say a special word about lilacs, because it seems to me that more questions are asked about hardening this shrub than any other. This is the way I have had the most success. First I strip off the leaves on the stem, leaving just one cluster near the flower head to help conduct water to it. Then I slit the stems for about three inches, and bang a hammer on the ends a few times, to increase the water-absorbing area, and put them in deep water overnight. After this treatment they usually last beautifully. I once cut three-foot branches of hybrid white lilacs in Massachusetts on a Tuesday, treated the stems as mentioned above, and put them in deep water in clean garbage cans. On Wednesday I put the cans in a station wagon and transported them to New Jersey. On Thursday I arranged them in hanging baskets for a wedding, and on Friday at the wedding they were as fresh and perky as though they were still on a bush.

Figure 2. The proper way to condition heavy shrubs. (Photo by Roche)

Bulbs, such as tulips, narcissus, and hyacinths, may have a beady drop of moisture on the end of the stem when you cut them. Wipe this away. Otherwise it will seal the end of the stem and prevent water from entering.

Some decorative foliage wilts quickly, but if you submerge it in water, preferably overnight, it will last for days. Do this for calla lily leaves, Japanese maple, hosta leaves, ivy leaves, begonia leaves, and the new growth of roses and peonies. Violets will keep best if you completely immerse them for a while.

Cut camellias, gardenias, and orchids do not need to be in water after they are cut, but they keep best when surrounded with moisture. Sprinkle them lightly, and put them on a bed of moist tissue in a box and keep them in a cool place.

It is not necessary to harden evergreens, although rhododendrons will be more graceful in an arrangement after several days hardening. Some people use oils or other preparations to shine the leaves of broad-leaved evergreens, but you can give them a very natural-looking shine by cleaning them with warm soapy water, and then rubbing them to a gloss with waxed paper.

You hear many theories about various formulas to put in water as you harden them to make them last longer. Whether or not they really do any good is a debatable question, but they don't do any harm. If someone passes a. pet theory on to you, go ahead and experiment. The chances are, though, that if your flowers are fresh, and they are put in fresh water, they will last the maximum time anyway. Also, well-hardened flowers should last as well arranged in a shallow bowl as in a deep one, providing that as the water evaporates you keep adding fresh. It isn't necessary to recut stems and completely change the water—in fact it is better not to, as the more flowers are handled the quicker they will wilt.

Place completed arrangements where they will be out of direct drafts and away from coal and gas fumes and the heat of fireplaces or stoves. Any of these things will shorten the life of plant material.

There are things that you can do to flowers and foliage as they are hardening to give them a different shape. Tulips are one of the most beautiful, but admittedly one of the most difficult flowers to

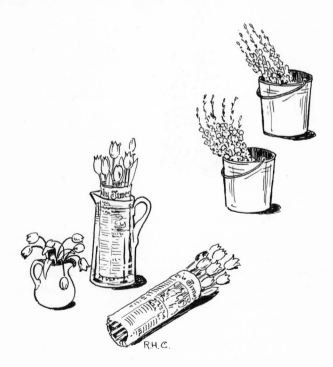

R.H.C.

Arrangement by Myra Brooks

Figure 3. This arrangement of early spring branches and tulips illustrates how each individual leaf and flower is an important part of the design. Note how the tulip at the focal point has been manually opened to make it a larger flower. (Photo by Roche)

arrange. If you want the stems to curve, they stand up straight—and if you want them straight, they invariably curve. You can manage them successfully if you pick or buy them in tight bud, and wrap the ones you want to be straight in a tube of newspaper, fastening it tightly around the stems right up to the flowers, with elastic bands. Soak them that way overnight in a tall container. Let the ones you want to curve hang over the side of the container while they are soaking. The flowers in the arrangement in Fig. 3 have been conditioned in this way.

If spiky flowers like snapdragons, lupines, and stock are ramrod straight and you want them to curve, put them in a pail or laundry tub to soak with the ends hanging over the edge at an angle. The tips will curve beautifully and they instinctively try and assume their vertical position.

Much stiff woody material like palm boots, palm spathes, cornhusks, and wisteria vine can be soaked in very hot water until it is supple, and then shaped into intriguing curves. Roots, branches, and heavy bark can actually be boiled to make them manageable. In fact, it's great fun to experiment. If there is something stiff and unwieldy that you want to shape, try boiling it.

Weathered wood and driftwood can be cleaned with a stiff brush, and used as it is, or if it is half peeled, you may want to peel the bark off altogether. You can get a bleached effect on wood by scrubbing it with a strong Chlorox solution.

If you have flowers that inexplicably wilt before you arrange them, there is a drastic treatment that will sometimes restore them. Protecting the flower heads with a towel or paper, plunge them into water as hot as your hand will stand and leave them until the water cools. This has worked for me with roses, carnations, and poinsettias.

PLANT MATERIAL ACCORDING TO SHAPE

Round	Spiky	Pendulant	Irregular
African Daisy	Artemisia	Acacia	Ageratum
Anemone	Astilbe	Billbergia	Amaryllis
Aster	Bridal Wreath	Bittersweet	Calla
Azalea	Broom	Bleeding Heart	Canna
Bachelor's Button	Campanula	Bougainvillaea	Columbine

Round	Spiky	Pendulant	Irregular
Begonia (tuberous)	Delphinium	Cup-and-Saucer Vine	Coralbell
Calendula	Flowering branches	Fuchsia	Daffodil
California Poppy	Forsythia	Golden Chain Tree	Day Lily
Camellia	Foxglove	Grapes	Easter Lily
Candytuft	Gladiolus	Honeysuckle	Forget-me-not
Carnation	Goldenrod	Jasmine	Freesia
Christmas Rose	Heather	Lantana	Fritillaria
Chrysanthemum	Hyacinth	Orchid	Grape Hyacinth
Cineraria	Larkspur	Pepper Berry	Gypsophila
Clarkia	Liatris	Smilax	Iris
Clematis	Lilac	Snowberry	Lily of the Valley
Cockscomb	Lupin	Trumpet Vine	Meadow Rue
Cosmos	Mock Orange	Wisteria	Narcissus
Crape Myrtle	Monkshood		Oleander
Dahlia	Pentstemon		Petunia
Daisy	Physostegia	*Foliage*	Plumbago
Dogwood	Poker Plant		Primula
Gaillardia	Salvia	Clematis	Rubrum Lily
Gardenia	Snapdragon	Grape Ivy	Sweet Pea
Geranium	Stock	Ivy	Tuberose
Godetia	Tamarix	Jade Plant	Tulip
Hibiscus	Thermopsis	Pothos	Viola
Hydrangea	Wallflower	Smilax	Violet
Magnolia	Weigela	Tradescantia	
Marguerite	Yucca		
Marigold			*Foliage*
Pansy			
Passion Flower	*Foliage*		Begonia (Angel Wing)
Peony			Begonia (Rex)
Poinsettia	Aspidistra		Caladium
Poppy	Canna		Coleus
Ranunculus	Croton		Maple
Rose	Dracaena		Philodendron
Salpiglossis	Iris		
Scabiosa	Narcissus		
Sweet William	Pandanus		
Tuberose	Sansevieria		
Tulip tree flower	Ti		
Zinnia			

Foliage

Begonia (Beefsteak)
Galax
Geranium
Hosta
Sea Grape

Below is a list of flowers that are usually stocked by a florist, which tells what months they are most apt to be in good supply. I have listed them in color ranges, so that if you are planning a certain color scheme you will have an idea of what is available for you to use.

The next time you are in a florist's shop, ask to see material on this list with which you are not familiar. A little study will pay great dividends in more unusual and distinctive arrangements.

I have purposely not included flowers to plant in a garden, because for anyone who is interested in growing flowers for arranging, there is a wealth of information in seed catalogues.

FLORISTS' FLOWERS

Pink through Red

Name	*When Obtainable*
African Daisy	Most Months
Amaryllis	Jan., Feb., March
Anemone	Jan., Feb., March, April, May, Nov., Dec.
Anthurium	Most Months
Aquilegia (Columbine)	May, June, July
Begonia	Dec., Jan.
Camellia	Jan., Feb., March, Nov., Dec.
Carnation	Most Months
China Aster	June, July, Aug., Sept., Oct., Nov., Dec.
Chrysanthemum	Most Months
Cockscomb (Celosia)	Aug., Sept.
Cornflower (pink)	Most Months

Pink through Red (cont.)

Name	When Obtainable
Dahlia	June, July, Aug., Sept.
Daphne	March, April
Gladiolus	Most Months
Heather	Jan., Feb., March, Nov., Dec.
Larkspur	June, July, Aug., Sept.
Orchid	Most Months
Peony	May, June
Rose	Most Months
Rubrum Lily	Jan., Feb., March, April, May, June, July, Aug., Sept.
Scabiosa	March, April, May, June, July, Aug., Sept.
Snapdragon	Most Months
Stock	Feb., March, April, June, July
Sweet Pea	Jan., Feb., March, May, June, July, Nov.
Tulip	Jan., Feb., March, April, May
Zinnia	May, June, Aug., Sept., Oct.

Blue, Lavender, Purple

Name	When Obtainable
Anemone	Jan., Feb., March, April, May, Nov., Dec.
Aquilegia (Columbine)	May, June, July
Blue Sage	June, July, Aug.
China Aster	June, July, Aug., Sept.
Chrysanthemum	Most Months
Cockscomb (Celosia)	Aug., Sept.
Cornflower	Most Months
Dahlia	June, July, Aug., Sept.
Delphinium	Jan., April, May, June, July, Aug.
Freesia	Jan., Feb., March, April, Dec.
Gladiolus	Most Months
Grape Hyacinth	Feb., March, April
Heather	Jan., Feb., March, Nov., Dec.
Iris	Jan., Feb., March, April, May
Japanese Iris	July
Lace Flower	Feb.
Larkspur	June, July, Aug., Sept.

Blue, Lavender, Purple (cont.)

Name	When Obtainable
Lilac	Feb., March, April, May
Lupin	May, June
Orchid	Most Months
Pansy	Jan., Feb., March, April, May, June, Dec.
Scabiosa	March, April, May, June, July, Aug., Sept.
Stock	Feb., March, April, May, June, July
Sweet Pea	Jan., Feb., March, May, June, July, Nov.
Tulip	Jan., Feb., March, April, May
Violet	Jan., Feb., March, April, May, Dec.

Yellow through Orange

Name	When Obtainable
Acacia	Jan., Feb., March
African Daisy	Most Months
Amaryllis	Jan., Feb., March
Aquilegia	May, June, July
Calendula	Jan., Feb., March, April
Calla Lily	Jan., Feb., March, April, May, June, Oct., Nov.
Carnation	Most Months
Chrysanthemum	Most Months
Cockscomb (Celosia)	Aug., Sept.
Daffodil	Jan., Feb., March, April, Dec.
Dahlia	June, July, Aug., Sept.
Forsythia	Feb., March, April
Freesia	Jan., Feb., March, April, Dec.
Gaillardia	June, Aug.
Gladiolus	Most Months
Iris	Jan., Feb., March, April, May
Lupine	May, June
Marigold	June, Aug., Sept.
Nasturtium	May, June, Aug.
Orchid	Most Months
Pansy	Jan., Feb., March, April, May
Poker Plant (Tritoma)	July, Aug., Sept., Oct.

Yellow through Orange (cont.)

Name	When Obtainable
Ranunculus	Jan., Feb., March, June, July, Nov., Dec.
Rose	Most Months
Snapdragon	Most Months
Stock	Feb., March, April, May, June, July
Strelitzia (Bird-of-Paradise)	Jan., Feb., March
Tulip	Jan., Feb., March, April, May
Zinnia	May, Aug., Sept., Oct.

White

Name	When Obtainable
African Daisy	Most Months
Anthurium	Feb., March, April, May, Nov., Dec.
Amaryllis	Jan., Feb.
Anemone	Jan., Feb., March, April, May, Nov., Dec.
Aquilegia (Columbine)	May, June, July
Begonia	Dec., Jan.
Bouvardia	Jan., Feb., Oct., Nov., Dec.
Calla Lily	Jan., Feb., March, April, May, Oct., Nov., Dec.
Camellia	Jan., Feb., March, Nov., Dec.
Carnation	Most Months
China Aster	June, July, Aug., Sept., Oct., Nov.
Chrysanthemum	Most Months
Dahlia	June, July, Aug., Sept.
Easter Lily	Feb., March, April
Eucharis Lily	July, August, Sept.
Freesia	Jan., Feb., March, April, Dec.
Gardenia	Most Months
Gladiolus	Most Months
Gypsophila (Baby's Breath)	April, May, June, July, Aug.
Japanese Iris	July
Larkspur	June, July, Aug., Sept.
Lilac	Feb., March, April, May
Lily of the Valley	Feb., March, April, May, June

White (cont.)

Name	When Obtainable
Marguerite	June, July, Aug.
Orchid	Most Months
Pansy	Jan., Feb., March, April, May, June
Paper-white Narcissus	Oct., Nov., Dec.
Rose	Most Months
Scabiosa	March, April, May, June, July, Aug., Sept.
Shasta Daisy	July, Aug., Sept.
Snapdragon	Most Months
Stephanotis	Feb., March, April, Oct., Nov.
Sweet Pea	Jan., Feb., Mar., May, June, July, Nov.
Stock	Feb., March, April, May, June, July
Tuberose	July, Aug., Sept., Oct., Nov.
Tulip	May, June, Aug., Sept., Oct.

MECHANICAL AIDS

HOW MANY times I have heard a woman say, "I love flowers. I know just how I want them to look in an arrangement, but they never end up that way. Everything falls apart." The very fact that she has a mental picture shows that this woman could be a good arranger. What she lacks is a knowledge of the mechanical aids that are so helpful in creating a finished picture. For luckily, just as there are things that help make cooking and sewing easier, so there are aids for flower arranging.

It *is* possible to beat the white of an egg to velvety peaks with a fork, but why do it when it is so much easier and more efficient to use a beater? You *can,* by balancing flowers in a container as carefully as though you are playing jackstraws, make a good arrangement. It is more likely, however, that as you carefully put the last stem in position, the delicate balance will be disturbed and the whole thing will tumble apart. This is when frustration sets in and you are ready to forget the whole thing. I know this, because often, when I offer to help a hostess, she will say, "Oh wonderful— you can fix the flowers," and then proceeds to hand me some flowers and a container, with either no mechanical aids or at best an inadequate pinholder.

Just as a cook has her drawers of cooking implements, and a seamstress her cabinet of sewing materials, a flower arranger also needs supplies and a definite place to keep them. I would suggest a sizable kitchen cupboard or drawer or shelf—for before we are through, you will see that the list is fairly long. Only someone who has worked for years with makeshift mechanics can appreciate the things that have come on the market in recent years to make flower arranging easy. Most of the things listed here are referred to many times in descriptions of arrangements, in this book, and it would be a very good idea to become familiar with them.

You will need:

It is best to have two pairs—one for cutting flowers (the kind *Shears* sold in a florist's shop or hardware store especially for this purpose is preferable) and another for cutting branches or wire. Keep them sharp, for a ragged cut from dull shears seals the stem of a flower and prevents it from getting proper moisture. After years of exasperation in losing my shears underneath material as I worked, I have finally learned to paint the handles bright red so that I can spot them easily.

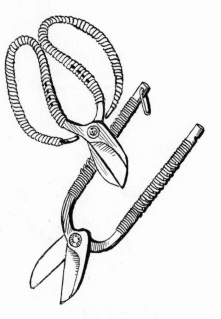

The most popular flower holder is a pinholder or, as it is some- *Flower* times called, needleholder. These come in many shapes and sizes, *Holders* and consist of a heavy metal base with sharp pins placed close together sticking up from it. (It doesn't pay to buy a cheap pinholder, for the space between the individual pins is too wide to be really efficient and the pins soon bend flat under the weight of any but the lightest stems.)

You can stick a flower stem firmly on the pins, and then bend it to any desired angle. Instead of hurting the flower, the points actually help it by piercing the stem and making it better able to absorb water.

Pinholders also come encased in a metal cup which holds water. You use this on a flat plate, a board, driftwood, or any container you can't fill with water. Because of the extra weight of the metal cup, it is also good for holding heavy branches. If you don't have a cup pinholder you can make one by fastening a regular pinholder in a tuna fish can or plastic cheese box with floral clay.

Another type of flower holder, good to use when stems need more support than is available in a pinholder, is a square cage

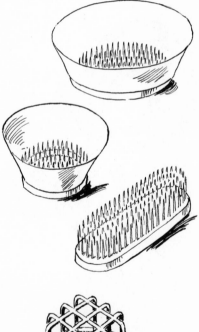

made of heavy wire. You can put the stems at any angle in the small openings in both the top and bottom of a holder like this, and they will be supported in both places. These holders also come with a pinholder attached to the bottom.

Remember that a flower holder must never show in your arrangement. You can cover it with leaves in the lower part of the arrangement, or with rocks, glass slag, pebbles, or similar things.

Many people, who do not realize its drawbacks, own a flower holder that is not recommended. This is one made of heavy glass with vertical holes in it. One reason that it is not successful is that the bottom is solid, and the flowers get only as much water as can be contained in the small individual opening. Another reason is that the holes have straight sides and hold the stems rigidly upright.

Although live plant material is not something you can keep in a kitchen drawer, no discussion of aids for holding flowers would be complete without explaining its use for "stuffing" a tall wide-mouthed vase. If you have such a vase, and who doesn't, you have undoubtedly found that any flowers you put in it fall toward the edge and lean on the rim for support, leaving the middle of the arrangement a blank hole. To make the flowers stay in position, completely fill the container with upright pieces of privet, fern,

yew, hemlock, or other greens. Cut off the ends level with the top of the vase. Now, when you insert the flower stems, they will stay where you want them.

Oasis

In recent years a boon to arrangers has come on the market in a material called Oasis. This is a block of porous material sold at florists' shops. It is feather light when dry, and very heavy when soaked. Use it wet, and soak it first for two or more hours so that it is thoroughly saturated. You won't need any other water in the container, although I usually keep a little in the bottom to insure the Oasis staying moist.

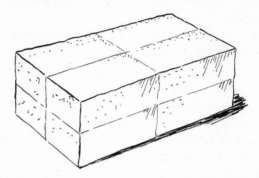

This is wonderful to use in a low wide-mouthed container like a Revere bowl or a soup tureen. Be sure and use a piece large enough to wedge against the sides of the container so that it won't slip. For a very firm foundation, for a large mass arrangement, anchor a pinholder to the bottom of the container with florist's clay, and press the block of Oasis down on it.

You can insert the flower stems directly into the block at any desired angle. If you want some flowers or foliage to hang down over the sides of the container, have the Oasis extend a half inch or so above the top of the container. Then you can push the stems of the flowers you want to hang over the edge up into the Oasis.

The only drawback to Oasis is that it is relatively expensive. However, after you have used it, you can put it on a newspaper to dry and use it again. When it is finally too full of holes to use again as a block, you can crumble it and use it for stuffing a tall vase.

You can also buy at florists' shops small round metal saucers with a round frame in the center, which holds a small round plug of Oasis that just fits the opening in the frame. These are most useful for small bouquets, centerpieces for individual tables, arrangements for coffee tables, etc.

No experienced arranger would be without a supply of these picks. They are short green sticks, individually wound with a piece of fine wire. You can buy them in different lengths at a florist's. It seems to me that I never do an arrangement without using at least one. For instance—suppose you are making a spring arrangement, and you want a group of violets at the base. I don't know of a pinholder with points fine enough to support the thin stem of a violet. However, with a florist's pick there is no problem. Just take several of the flowers, hold them against the pick, and wind the wire firmly around the stems. Insert the strong stick into the pinholder, where it will support the flowers, but will be hidden behind them. Or perhaps you are using carnations, and the relatively weak stems bend with the weight of the top-heavy flowers. Wire a pick to the carnation stem, and its support will hold the stem upright.

Picks are used in fruit arrangements to fasten different pieces of fruit together. Before the days of picks, it was much more difficult to make wreaths and swags, for everything had to be wired individually into the background material. Now the cones, fruit, ribbons, and other component parts are wired to picks and then the picks just stuck in the greens or Styrofoam you are using as a base.

Water picks are almost as useful in arranging as florist's picks. These are little plastic tubes, tapering down to a wedge, topped with rubber caps with a hole in the center. These are filled with water, and are used to hold material that would otherwise be out of water. If there is just one flower, you can stick the stem through the hole in the cap, and it will be held in place. If you are using a cluster of stems, you can remove the cap.

Suppose you want some green leaves in a fruit arrangement. You can put them in one of these picks and stick the pointed end among the fruit, and the leaves will stay fresh. If you want to use some flowers with a piece of driftwood, you can put the flowers in water picks, wedge them into joints in the wood, and conceal them with a leaf. There will be other instances in descriptions of arrangements in the book where these picks are mentioned.

Florist's Clay   Pinholders, wonderful as they are, will sometimes slip if they are not fastened to the container. One way to do this is with a substance called florist's clay. This comes in a small roll and you can buy it at a florist's shop. You can soften it by molding it in your hands, and use it over and over again.

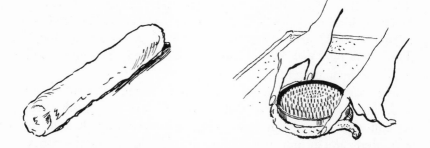

To fasten a pinholder to the bottom of a container, roll a piece of clay between the palms of your hands until it makes a "worm." Then, making sure that both container and pinholder are perfectly dry, press the roll of clay around the edge of the pinholder onto the container.

It has many other uses—plugging a small hole in a container so that it won't leak, filling in an uneven place in a container to make it level, so that the pinholder won't tip—mending a broken stem. Again, more uses are mentioned later.

Florist's clay will tarnish silver, so if you are using a silver container, use either Stickum or paraffin, as mentioned below.

I like this very much, because it is absolutely adhesive. However, it is quite a bit more expensive than florist's clay. This substance is flattened into a strip about half an inch wide, backed by waxed paper, and formed into a large roll like a roll of tape. You can unwind as much as you need, strip off the paper, and use it as you would clay. It seems absolutely slip proof, and anything fastened with it stays in place as though it were glued. You can remove all traces of it, though, with gasoline or naphtha.

Stickum

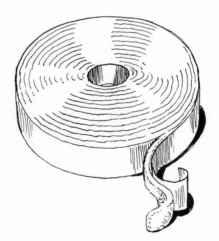

It is useful for fastening pieces of driftwood together, fastening water picks to driftwood, plugging holes, fastening candles in holders, and many, many other uses (including fastening on my husband's false mustache last Hallowe'en). This is available at florists' shops.

For a silver or a pewter container, when you want to fasten a pinholder, you can use paraffin. I always keep a few ends of used candles in my flower arranging drawer for this purpose. Melt

Paraffin and Candle Ends

the candles (or a block of paraffin) in a pan, and let it cool until it is slightly thickened. Make sure that both container and holder are dry. Then put the pinholder in place, and pour the wax over the edge of the pinholder where it joins the container.

Some of the most elegant flower containers are made of alabaster. Many an arranger has found to her sorrow that alabaster disintegrates on contact with water. If you are fortunate enough to have an alabaster vase, epergne, or compote, pour some melted paraffin in it and gently turn it until all surfaces that will come in contact with water are coated.

Drops of paraffin in the center of a water lily will keep it from closing. You can have a passionflower stay open to use in a corsage, or to float in a bowl, by dipping it quickly face down into melted paraffin. Be sure that it is tepid temperature. Immediately after dipping it into the paraffin, dip it into a bowl of ice water to harden the wax.

Pill Bottles and Long Sticks

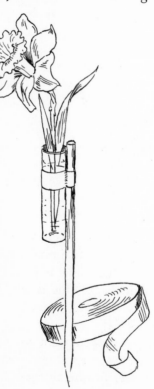

By all means save dark green or clear glass tubular pill bottles for your flower arranging drawer. They are often used with long green sticks (available at a florist's) or straight sturdy twigs from trees or shrubs to remedy a seemingly impossible situation.

Suppose for instance you are making an arrangement using a tall spiky form like delphinium or stock for the highest point. You accidentally break the stem and you have no other to take its place. All is not lost. Simply tape, wire, or fasten with Stickum a pill bottle to a strong stick, put water in the bottle and the broken stalk in the water. Cut the stick to a length to compensate for the broken stem, and you're all set. (Of course cover the bottle and any part of the stick that shows with other flowers or leaves.)

A stick-supported tube can hold a small bunch of flowers at a desired place in an arrangement much higher than their normally short stems will allow. This is especially valuable with the short-stemmed leaves of houseplants like angel wing or rex begonias that you might want to use at a focal point.

Wire

In your flower arranging drawer you should have several spools of wire, ranging from fine to heavy. You will find innumerable uses for it. Fine wire is used to fasten small-stemmed flowers such as violets, lilies of the valley, or sweet peas in bunches if you want to group them for an arrangement. You use it for wiring flowers for corsages, and for wiring greens into bunches for roping and garlands.

If you want pussy willow, Scotch broom, podocarpus, or similar material to curve in certain directions, you can bend it into the desired shape, fasten it with wire, and let it stand overnight in water. When you remove the wire, the material will usually stay in the form in which you have bent it.

Cellophane Tape

This also has many uses in the flower arranging world. Probably all of us remember putting the stem of a dandelion in our mouths to make it curl at the end, when we were children. It isn't as much fun when you are making an arrangement of daffodils or narcissus and the stems curl in the water the same way. It makes it almost impossible to put them on a pinholder. If you fasten a piece of tape around the base of such stems before you put them on the pinholder, it will prevent them from doing this.

Tulip leaves can be very contrary. You can make them behave if you tape a piece of fine wire to the back of the leaf. Then, with the help of the wire, you can make the leaf bend in the direction you want.

Florist's Tape

This is a narrow, somewhat sticky green tape that comes in a small roll.

If you are using a needleholder in a glass bowl, and don't have

a cup type that conceals the needles, you can wind tape around the outside of the needles to hide their brightness and keep them from being magnified by the glass.

This tape is used to wrap the wire stems of dried material, or flowers for corsages. It can mend a broken stem or leaf, or fasten tubes on sticks.

Chicken Wire

When you are making arrangements in a number of wide-mouthed containers (such as for a church supper or other community activity) and you don't want to spend the money for pin-holders or Oasis, crumpled chicken wire makes an adequate filler to hold flower stems.

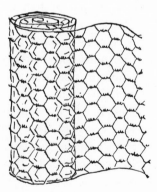

If possible, though, fasten it to the bottom of the container with lumps of clay or Stickum, as otherwise the wire is apt to slip around as you are working.

This is a heavy wire mesh with square openings. You can use *Hardware* it as a basis for wreaths and swags, cutting it into any desired *Cloth* shape, and wiring whatever decorative material you wish on it. For instance, if you wanted a garlanded swag for a mantle at Christmas, you could cut the hardware cloth into the exact shape you want, and proceed from there.

Sometimes it is hard to know how to put a very large branch like pine or driftwood onto a pinholder. The wood is too hard for the needles to penetrate. If you cut a strip of hardware cloth, and tack it around the end of the branch, with an inch or so extending over the edge, you can insert this extension into the pins of the holder.

Every year I learn something new in the way of mechanical *Tin Wedge* aids. This year it was wedge holders, which were described to *Holders* me by a charming woman from Portugal. She said that their high-

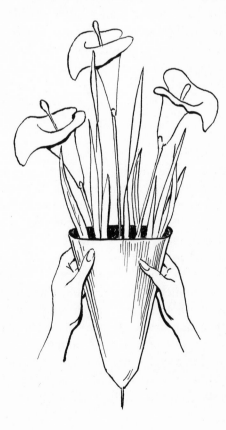

ceilinged rooms call for very tall arrangements, and to get extra height they use flat tin cones painted green. These are filled with flowers, and thrust among those already in a container to build the arrangement to greater heights.

These would also be useful if you wanted to dress up your garden for a special occasion by filling them with flowers and sinking them into the earth at strategic points among the foliage plants.

Hand Lotion Any flower arranger worth her salt ends up with grimy hands. An on-the-spot application of some hand cream will save hard scrubbing later.

Books Every flower arranger should have on hand a good garden encyclopedia and a book on wildflowers. If you work with flowers you should know them by name, and a little study will soon make you familiar with them. If someone says "Why not use astilbe for height?" or "Some hemerocallis would be good at the focal point," you will know what they are talking about. Also you will know what flowers to plant, and what to ask for at a florist's.

By studying wildflowers, you will get to know which ones grow in profusion and which ones are rare. Rare plants should not be picked, except where an area is to be developed, and they may be destroyed.

No arrangement can be successful without a firm foundation, and while it is easy to do this in most cases by using some of the aids described above, sometimes you have to be resourceful and work out a special problem. For example, in the arrangement in the lamp base container that is described in the chapter on Containers, I was faced with several problems. The container was a bronze lamp base on three curved legs. A sizable hole in the bottom prevented it from holding water. I wanted to use apple blossoms whose branches were tall and thick—too heavy for Oasis. If I plugged the hole in the bottom, and used a heavy pinholder, it would be so far below the rim of the container that I couldn't slant the branches for a good design.

This is the way I solved it. I discovered that two coffee cans would just fill the bowl of the lamp base. One I inverted, and fastened the bottoms of the cans together with Stickum. In the top can I fastened a heavy pinholder, and filled the can with water. The can on the bottom raised the level of the top one to a point where I could fasten the branches in the pinholder vertically, and then slant them in the direction I wanted. By putting the water only in the top can, it wasn't necessary to do anything about the hole in the bottom of the container.

No matter what you use as a mechanical aid, it should always be hidden. Just as you close the kitchen door to hide the pots and pans you used to cook a gourmet dinner, and put away the vacuum cleaner that helped put your house in perfect order, you also conceal the mechanical means by which you have made a lovely arrangement.

CONTAINERS AND BASES

M ANY beautiful vases, or containers, as they are usually called
in flower arranging circles, are sold especially to hold flowers. However, you are not limited to these. Sometimes it is an object designed for another purpose that is the most attractive and
the most fun to use. You might have an antique china or pewter
sugar bowl, a copper pitcher, a Bristol glass perfume bottle, a
footed water goblet, a wooden or metal box, a Tole bread tray, or
a teakettle like the one in Fig. 5. Or you might have a natural
object like a conch shell or a piece of driftwood. Any of these
lends its own interest to an arrangement.

Looking for interesting containers should appeal to people who
like to go antiquing. Some of the most treasured ones come from
antique shops, and I don't necessarily mean valuable and expensive china and porcelain. For instance, if you ever come across
an urn-shaped ornamental Victorian stove top, grab it. Inverted,
it makes a footed urn that you will find just right for many types
of arrangements.

You might find an antique perfume bottle that you can buy
for very little, because it is minus a stopper. Often you will find
a tall tea caddy. Instead of making it into a lamp, keep it for tall
flowers like flowering fruit branches, lilac, and forsythia. An old
soup tureen makes a wonderful container for the dining room
table, and the plain white ironstone ones look well with many
patterns of china. You may even find a chipped Victorian vase
that would be very expensive if it were undamaged. You can get
it cheaply and hide the chipped place with some leaves. The

Figure 4. Some household objects which are suitable and interesting to use as flower containers are pictured above. They are, from left to right, glass bottle, pewter sugar bowl, pewter pipe holder, glass goblet, old glass toothpick holder, pottery bottle, tole bread tray, ironstone sugar bowl, old glass spoonholder, Chinese teacup, basket, glass utensil, driftwood, pottery bottle, and shell. (Photo by Roche)

fluted white saucers known as "smoke bells" that hung over the gaslights in our grandmothers' day are just the thing for a nosegay bouquet.

Try to become aware of commercial containers that would make interesting vases. One winter on a ship going to South America we had some Chilean wine at the table. The bottles were such a lovely shade of green and such a fascinating squat shape that I couldn't bear to think of them being thrown out, so I asked the steward to save them for me. At the time I had no idea what I would do with them. Now, filled with sprays of tradescantias, they make a stunning hall decoration. They are placed on dark green brackets, hung asymetrically against the wall.

Be on the lookout at rummage and white elephant sales for containers that may be hideous in color, and too "busy" in decoration, but are of basically good design. You can often buy them for a few pennies. Take them home and paint them with a good flat paint. You can use any color, but my favorite is called Satin Black. This gives a very dull smooth finish and, by subordinating everything to the basically good design, transforms an ugly vase into an elegant one.

Flowers and containers must never compete for interest. Each should .complement the other for a harmonious effect. For this reason, it is more difficult to use a container that is strong in color, or is heavily decorated. The happiest choices are potteries in neutral shades of white, gray brown, and soft green, or metals such as iron, pewter, copper, or brass. Black is always a good color, and like the "basic black dress" fits many occasions.

Every flower arranger should have a favorite container—one for which she finds many uses, and one which never fails to inspire her. I have two—and I didn't search for either of them. They just happened. The first one is the alabaster epergne pictured in Plate 5.

Each year an antique show is held at our church, and some of us make arrangements to decorate the booths. One evening at the close of the show I was collecting my things and saw one of the dealers packing an alabaster epergne. It was love at first sight. I thought, "Oh, I must have that," never dreaming it would be in my price range. Evidently, though, the dealer was tired, and it would be one less thing to lug back to his store, for he quoted me a ridiculously low figure, and the epergne was mine.

Arrangement by Myra Brooks

Figure 5. The choice of an unusual container gives distinction to this arrangement of familiar marigolds, zinnias, and high-bush cranberry. (Photo by Roche)

This is a "special occasion" container. I have used it for many exhibits in flower shows with fruit or flowers, and it has been a "guest" at numerous parties. Arranged with live greens and cascading Christmas tree ornaments, as in Plate 5, it has become as much a part of our usual Christmas as the tree, and if I try to skip a year the family protests. For each of my daughters' weddings, instead of a tiered wedding cake, I had a large round one made with a hole in the center. The base of the epergne fitted in the hole, and its tiers, decorated with gardenias, stephanotis, and tiny ivy acted as tiers for the cake.

My other favorite container, which I use every day, I discovered out of desperation. I had been invited to do an arrangement for a large State Flower Show which was in the form of an "Open Homes Show." My assignment was in the country house of an internationally famous hostess. I was told to do an arrangement on the piano in the large living room. The specifications said that an original Renoir in shades of pink and rose hung over the piano, and it was flanked by two armchairs covered in dull gold satin.

Frankly, I was at my wit's end. I knew that the arrangement must be tall, that it must complement and not compete with the picture, and that the container must be beautiful and distinctive. I didn't have one that I thought was just right, and I didn't want to go out and buy one. One day I came into the garage and stumbled over a large black object. It was a metal lamp and shade. When my husband, who had been clearing out his father's attic, brought it home I took one quick look and said, "Ugh—take it away." Now, as I moved it out of my way, I noticed the shape of the base and thought, "That looks quite interesting." I removed the top and shade, and took the base in the house and started to polish it. I discovered that it was bronze, with a lovely soft patina. As the accumulation of dirt and grime was removed, the raised pattern of a bird sitting on a flowering spring branch emerged. With each rub of the polishing cloth I was more thrilled, and when finally it was finished, it was beautiful! I had my distinctive container. Not only that, but the decoration of the flowering branch gave me a clue for the arrangement. I would use apple blossoms.

I did just that—making a line arrangement, whose branching arms framed the picture without competing with it. For a focal

point I used deep pink Martha Washington geraniums. The pink color of the flowers was reflected in the bronze, giving it a rosy cast that was truly lovely.

However, the best part is that from that day the container has been in constant use in my own living room. Even empty it is

53

lovely, but as you can see from the drawing on page 53 it lends itself to any type of arrangement—line, line mass, and mass. And this brings up an important point. Some people feel that it is necessary to have many containers so that they can do different kinds of arrangements. This is not true. I think it is more satisfactory to have a few containers that really appeal to you, and look well in your room. Learn to do different types of arrangements in them. You can plan the mechanics so that you always know how you will anchor your flowers, and not have to spend time figuring out a new way for each different vase.

In flower arranging classes, I have asked pupils to bring containers that they find a problem to use, and they have brought three types so consistently that I think they must be problems to many. In each case the proper "mechanics" is the answer.

The first of these types is the tall wide-mouthed vase, designed as an ornament in itself, that I call "the wedding present vase," because almost every bride is given one.

Such a one is pictured in Fig. 6. Because of the wide mouth of the container any flowers placed in it fall toward the rim of the vase, giving a very top-heavy effect and making the creation of a good design practically impossible. It is necessary to find some way to make the flower stems stay where you want them. In the one pictured here, this is done by wedging a piece of Oasis into the wide part of the container, until it is held firmly by the narrower part of the vase. You could also do this by filling the container with straight pieces of privet or other material as described in Part I under "Mechanical Aids." Once you know that your flower stems will stay where you place them, you can plan your design.

The second type that seems to give difficulty is the glass vase —either a tall one, or a glass bowl. People want to know how to hide stems and pinholders. In the case of the tall glass vase, it isn't necessary to hide the stems. You can make them part of the picture.

You won't need a pinholder. Instead, cut a piece of fine chicken wire a little larger than the top of the vase, and bend the edges down over the rim. Stripping off any foliage that will be below the water line, slip the stems through the holes, and the mesh will hold them in place. Be sure to conceal the wire with foliage. Also be sure to have some of the stems touch the bottom of the

Arrangement by
Katherine N. Cutler
Vase courtesy
Lenox China

Figure 6

BEFORE

In this arrangement in an ornamental vase of fine china typical of the one often received as a wedding present or other gift, the flowers and vase do not complement each other in design. The creamy stock is a good choice in color and texture, but there is otherwise no integration of flowers and container. (Photo by Roche)

AFTER

Because of the strong vertical lines and bold vertical curves of the vase, a modified vertical design is indicated for the flower arrangement. Placing the vase on an antique Chinese base gives it weight and stability, thus permitting the arrangement to have dramatic height. A wedge of Oasis forced into the wide neck of the vase holds the flower stems in position so that they don't fall to the edges. We have used the same flowers as in the first picture but have added branches of camellia foliage to strengthen the vertical line. The glossy leaves further accentuate the glaze of the container. The stock is cut in varying lengths with the full stalks centered vertically and the buds used to make interesting voids. Some of the foliage is curved over the neck of the vase to further coordinate flowers and container. (Photo by Roche)

container, or the flowers will look as though they are floating in space. Place the other flowers so that groups of stems touch each side of the vase, making a triangular pattern with the ones at the bottom. Immerse a pretty cluster of leaves below the water line. Now, although you can see the stems, they form a pleasing part of the whole arrangement.

If the glass container is a low bowl, the problem is a little harder because you will have to hide a pinholder. To do this, line the bottom of the bowl, while it is dry, with dry leaves like rose, ivy, or chrysanthemum leaves, letting a few come up the side to hide the pinholder. Then, making sure that it is also dry, fasten a *cup* pinholder (if you use a regular one, some of the pins may show and be magnified through the glass) to the bottom with clay. An arrangement in a low glass bowl is shown in Plate 10.

The third difficult type is the high wide-mouthed bowl like a Revere bowl. Usually the large bowl is to be used for a mass arrangement on a table, and what seems to bother people is how to fill the cavity from one pinholder low in the center. In this case I definitely recommend using Oasis. A mass arrangement in this type bowl is one of the easiest of all arrangements to do successfully, *if* you use a large block of Oasis. Not only can you insert flower stems in the center, but toward the edges of the bowl as well, and if the Oasis is a little higher than the rim, by inserting the stems up at an angle, you can have some of the flowers swooping gracefully at the sides.

If you don't have Oasis, and want to use a pinholder, you can be successful if you get a *large* pinholder, or one of the large cage-type holders described in Part I under "Mechanical Aids," and fasten it *firmly* in place. If you have such a bowl that you use often, and you don't want to depend on having Oasis on hand, shop for a pinholder that is really right for it and leave it fastened in place so that the container will always be ready to use.

If a vase is not footed, it is amazing to see how often putting it on a base will improve the design. Also, a base gives visual weight to the container, which allows you to make the arrangement taller. Scroll bases, like the one pictured in Plate 2, come in different sizes. Chinese bases like the ones pictured in Figs. 3 and 34 also are obtainable in different sizes. There are rectangular or circular boards, painted black or finished in natural wood colors, as well as boards in free form design. But you are by no means limited to these basic types. There are countless other things to use—iron or brass trivets, mirrors, pieces of slate, wood burls, bamboo mats, inverted plates, inverted porringers, flat slabs of coral, and many, many others.

There is a pair of bases that never fails to remind me that sometimes flower arrangers are legitimate prey for cartoonists. Recently I was planning an arrangement for an important show, using a pair of black urns. I wanted to place them on cylindrical black bases of different heights, and asked my husband if he could make them for me. He said, "Yes, but I think it would be better to find two cans of vegetables or fruit the proper size, and I'll paint them for you. Then they will not only be the right size, but they will be good and heavy."

I agreed that this was a good idea and set off for the supermarket, urn in hand. I was so intent on my problem that I was utterly unconscious of the picture I made—walking slowly down the aisle, taking a can from the shelf, picking the urn out of my basket, putting the urn on the can, shaking my head, and putting the can back on the shelf, until I looked up and saw a little knot of people looking at me in amazement. However, I did find the proper ones, one of tomato juice and one of sweet potatoes, and they repose on my container shelf in satiny black splendor.

COLLECTING ACCESSORIES FOR
ARRANGEMENTS

ONE OF the fascinating side lines of flower arranging is "collecting." Most of us have an acquisitive instinct, and the woods and beaches are full of wonderful things for the flower arranger to find. As we have said, mechanical aids are invaluable but must be hidden. A container often looks better if it is placed on a base. An accessory can add interest and distinction to an arrangement. For all these purposes, natural objects are often better than anything you can buy. There is a wealth of dried material just waiting to be picked up and make its appearance in a distinctive arrangement, and natural objects—driftwood, stumps, roots, and large shells—to be used as containers. The base in the arrangement in Fig. 7 is a slab cut from a cedar tree, and the main line of the composition was one of its dead branches.

I have some shelves in the garage—it might as well be in a pantry, basement, or utility room—where I keep my collection. Apart from being useful, these things never cease to remind me of happy times when I found them. There are jars of smooth pebbles, white, pink, gray, and black, gathered during daily walks on the beach. These are useful for concealing pinholders and for holding bulbs in place when they are growing indoors in a bowl. It is quite usual to use white pebbles for this, but have you ever thought of the dramatic effect of paper-white narcissus in a low white bowl surrounded by coal black pebbles, or pink hyacinths held in place by silvery gray stones in a pewter container? Incidentally, it is wise to gather things on the beach when you see them, for I didn't realize until I lived at the seashore that the sea is not consistent in giving up its treasures. One day the beach

Arrangement by Katherine N. Cutler

Figure 7. The rhythmic lines of a dead cedar branch are accented by a banana blossom and curled banana leaves. The base is a cedar slab. (Photo by Thomas W. Hall, Bermuda)

may be covered with white pebbles, and then you may see only scattered ones for days; their place has been taken by blue and black mussel shells, or tiny white clamshells.

On my shelf there are jagged pieces of slag, useful for concealing pinholders and adding color and design to an arrangement. One is black, shot with streaks of turquoise and rust. This came from the site of an iron furnace in the Berkshires which, legend has it, supplied the iron for guns of the *Monitor* in the Civil War. Other pieces I found on a municipal dump near a factory where glass Christmas tree balls are made. Some of these pieces are like rock candy, and others look like foaming blue-green tropical water that has been caught in motion and solidified. Some jagged chunks of Venetian glass, like emeralds and topazes, my sister picked up for me on the floor of a glass factory in Venice.

Some large stones with a smooth patina of age, that provide just the right note at the base of an arrangement of pine branches,

I picked up on walks by a mountain brook. There are pieces of silvery gray driftwood from New Jersey, large pine cones from California, embryo coconuts and boatlike coconut spathes from Florida. There is sand flecked with pink coral from a beach in Bermuda, and a triangular piece of coral that fell at my feet from a retaining wall there. Also from Bermuda are bags of casuarina cones—tiny perfect cones less than half an inch long that come from the casuarina trees planted all over the island to replace the blighted cedars—and rattail cones, long and slender, that can be bent into fascinating shapes before they dry.

In the past few years we have had the good fortune to do quite a bit of traveling. We leave with respectable, conventional luggage—but our return! We go by ship, and when our luggage is placed on the pier, it is surrounded by paper shopping bags, straw valises, cartons—anything that will hold the results of my "collecting." Also, my husband has become accustomed to the fact that we not only have to have a customs inspector, but an agricultural one as well. While he and the customs inspector attend to the regular luggage, the agricultural inspector and I go into a huddle. He sorts carefully through my treasures, confiscating some, but letting me keep most of them. Once one of them held up a coconut spathe and said, "What on earth are you going to do with this?" Already visualizing the arrangement in Plate 9, I launched into a description complete with gestures. He looked at me quizzically for a minute, thrust it in my hand and said, "Here, take it and have fun!"

As the result of a Mediterranean trip last spring, I have added to my collection of smooth white stones—but these are very special ones of sparkling marble, picked up on the beach of the island of Delos in Greece. I have pieces of pink granite from the ruins in Baalbek, and yellow sandstone taken from the desert in front of the Sphinx. On a visit to a kibbutz in Israel, I found some large round flat pods under a tree that I had never seen before, and on the campus of the American University in Beirut, I gathered the peanut-shaped pods of the mescal bean tree. I also have some stiff cones from a cedar of Lebanon, and some small round smooth hard ones from a tree on the island of Malta. All of these pods and cones will be in my Christmas wreath this year.

The bases on my shelf include a free-form piece of slate that

I must confess I stole when a neighbor was making a new terrace. I just couldn't resist its unusual shape. There is cork from the beach, and a polished burl from California.

These are some of the things I have found. Many more are all around, just waiting to be discovered. And once you start collecting, you will seldom return from an outing empty-handed. There is one thing, though. It does pay to keep your "collecting shelves" in order. Otherwise, things get in such a jumble that you either throw things away in sheer annoyance or are unable to find something when you need it most.

I keep small stones sorted by color in glass jars. Larger stones and slag are placed together on the open shelf. Cones, sorted by size, are hung in heavy shopping bags from nails. Driftwood and stumps have their place on the shelves. Small shells, sorted by size, are in plastic-lined berry boxes. Branches of dried material are tied with heavy twine and hung from nails. Because the jars, shopping bags, and berry boxes all have wide openings and there

Arrangement by Linda Browning

Figure 8. The flowing lines of the broom are accented by those of the figurine in this charming arrangement of broom, holly, carnation foliage, and chrysanthemums. The accessory is also related in color to the flowers and in texture to the glossy holly foliage. (Photo by Roche)

are no lids to remove, it is simple when you come in with something you have collected just to drop it in its proper place.

In addition to natural accessories, be on the lookout for figurines, statuettes, or pieces of sculpture that are decorative, and when used properly can dramatize an arrangement. The porcelain one in Fig. 8 is lovely in itself, and is an important feature of the arrangement as a whole.

II
Different Kinds of Arrangements

JAPANESE FLOWER ARRANGEMENTS

THE ART of flower arranging has been reverently studied by the Japanese for over a thousand years. It is part of their philosophy and religion. There are many schools, each with its own way of interpreting artistic values and moral doctrines, and the teachers and masters of these schools have always been among the most respected people.

They have contributed incalculably to the art. It is safe to say that we have never equaled the Japanese in perfection of arrangements, but they have taught us much. One of the greatest lessons is to appreciate the beauty in nature—the grace of curving branches, the joy of unfolding buds, and the serenity of stones and water. All of the Japanese schools teach students to revere nature, and use the full cycle of growth. One arrangement may have in it a plant in all stages from the tiniest bud to the dead end of a branch. They have taught us to bring outdoors inside. With as little as two buds and one flower, a few stones, some moss and water, we can have the feeling of a tiny garden in the house.

The three main lines used in the classic-style Japanese arrangement form the basis for many of ours. Japanese students think nothing of spending a whole day shaping the curved branches that form these three lines. We find it more expedient to choose ones that are already growing in the proper direction.

These branches (they can be leaves, or other material) are known as heaven, man, and earth. "Heaven" is the tallest, and is placed with its tip over the center of the arrangement, pointing upward. "Man" is approximately two-thirds the height of "heaven,"

Arrangement by Mrs. Harold Brooks

Figure 9. The Japanese have been responsible for showing us how attractive flowers are when they are arranged as they grow with natural stones and water as part of the design. This is beautifully illustrated in the above arrangement of a few tulips and narcissus, with their leaves. Notice how the petals of the tulip at the focal point have been turned back to make a larger and different flower form. Natural stones are used to hide the pinholder. (Photo by Roche)

and is placed close to the side of "heaven," also looking upward. "Earth" is the shortest, one-third the size of "man," and is placed low and facing forward, its tip also pointing up. You can see this placement in the step-by-step drawings on page 70, in the quince branches in Plate 2, and the tulip leaves in Fig. 9.

These three lines are often used as a complete arrangement. They can be branches, like pine, or lighter branches like pussy willow or broom which have been manipulated into the proper curves. (The method for doing this is described in Part II under "Foliage Arrangements.") The lines are often represented, too, by large single leaves like aspidistra, canna, ti, or sansevieria. This arrangement is particularly effective in an Oriental container, like the footed, flat-topped usabata, but is also successful in a shallow rectangular or oval container. Because of its simplicity and graceful beauty, this arrangement looks well in a room of almost any period.

For a fuller arrangement, each main line can have supporting lines, called "helpers," which follow the main line in form but are shorter. All the lines should come together at the bottom, like the trunk of a tree, so that they look as though they are growing from one spot. The supporting lines can be flowers, as shown in the step-by-step drawing.

You can see that many of our line arrangements are done in the Japanese manner. I say "manner" advisedly, because they are not true Japanese arrangements, but reflect their teachings. Even in mass arrangements, you can usually find a "heaven," "man," and "earth" line. In the drawing in Part I under "Principles of Design in Flower Arranging," you can see that they are represented by three flower stalks that make the pattern for the asymmetrical triangle which is typical of a Japanese arrangement.

You do not have to become a serious student of Japanese arrangement to have your own arrangements more beautiful. If you merely develop their awareness of nature, and become conscious of the strong foundation lines in their arrangements, you will be well on the road to creating lovely flower pictures.

FOLIAGE ARRANGEMENTS

P ROBABLY the greatest wealth of material available to a flower
arranger whether she lives East, West, North or South—in a
city, village, town, or open country—is foliage. Leaves and branches
from trees, bushes, vines and houseplants come in so many shapes,
sizes, colors, and textures that the possibilities for interesting arrangements are endless.

From earliest spring when the first curling shoots of ferns and
skunk cabbage appear in the woods until late fall when the last
oak leaves fall from the trees, there is a great variety and abundance—and all through the winter there are countless beautiful
evergreens available.

You can use branches of beech, oak, maple, or hickory, or purchase exotic foliage from foreign lands imported by your florist.
You may have a bouquet from your Northeastern dooryard of
laurel, andromeda, ivy, or juniper, a semitropical roadside combination of sansevieria, loquat leaves, and screw pine like the one
in Fig. 24, or one from the vegetable garden of rhubarb, kale, cabbage, spinach, or beet leaves. Houseplants, too, are a never-end-
ing source, with the tall leaves of aspidistra, sansevieria, or dracaena
often forming the basis of a striking arrangement, and begonia,
philodendron, or cyclamen leaves making a focal point.

Although we are apt to think of foliage as green, and it is true
that much of it is in that shade, there is much in a surprisingly
wide color range. We are all familiar with yellow, scarlet, and
orange maple leaves, the golden ones of hickory, and the red and
bronze ones of oak. But many others combine these colors with
green. Here is a list of some:

Yellow and Orange	Bronze	Violet	Red	White
Coleus	Andromeda	Canna	Azalea	Caladium
Croton	Beech	Coleus	Beet	Dieffenbachia
Pothos	Galax	Hydrangea	Begonia	Dracaena
Sansevieria	Juniper	Ti	Coleus	Euphorbia
Variegated Euonymous	Leucothoe	Tradescantia	Dogwood	Holly
Variegated Privet	Magnolia		Echeveria	Hosta
Pandanus	Mahonia		Peony	Tradescantia
	Peony		Rose	Variegated Holly
	Sea Grape			Variegated Ivy
	Hydrangea			Pandanus

Sometimes you will be thrilled and surprised to come across an unexpected color. This happened to me this fall, when I discovered some leaves on a hydrangea plant that were a beautiful clear bright blue.

You can also find the same forms, spiky, round, irregular, and pendulant that are used for flower arrangements. Some examples of these are:

Round and Heart-shaped	Spiky	Pendulant	Irregular
Cabbage	Aspidistra	Clematis	Begonia (several varieties)
Cyclamen	Broom	Grape Ivy	Ivy
Eucalyptus	Canna	Ivy	Maple
Galax	Dracaena	Ivy Geranium	Nephthytis
Geranium	Fern	Kangaroo Vine	Philodendron (several varieties)
Hen and Chickens	Iris	Passion Vine	
Hosta	Juniper	Philodendron	
Pothos	Palm	Pothos	
Sea Grape	Pittosporum	Smilax	
Violet	Podocarpus	Tradescantia	
	Sansevieria		
	Ti		
	Yucca		

STEP-BY-STEP
ARRANGEMENT

When you cut foliage from your plants for arrangements, you are really helping them, because proper pruning not only improves the shape of the plant, but is beneficial to its growth. Select branches that will fit in your visualized arrangement. You will find the ones with the most interesting shape at the bottom of bushes and trees, as they grow reaching for the light. Cut them with a sharp instrument, so that you don't leave a jagged area that is susceptible to decay.

If you live in an area where the winter is severe, I find it is best to cut foliage whose leaves curl or get brittle, like rhododendron and holly, before extreme cold. It will last a long time in water, particularly if you keep it in a cool place.

As with flowers, foliage should be put in deep water for several hours before arranging. Some leaves like to be completely immersed—in fact this helps all leaves—so if you are doubtful as to whether or not a particular one needs it, go ahead and cover it with water in your sink or laundry tub. Some that definitely *do* need this treatment are Japanese maple, calla lily, ivy, new rose shoots, new peony shoots, palm, and fern.

If you wish tall sweeping curves as the basis for your arrangement, foliage can be manipulated prior to using it. Bend sprays such as podocarpus or broom in the direction you wish, fasten the bends with wire, and leave them in water overnight. When you remove the wire, the sprays will curve in the desired direction. Gently bend leaves such as aspidistra, iris, or sansevieria, massaging them along the center with your fingertips. The heat from your hand will make them pliable. Smaller leaves like narcissus or tulip leaves can be curled around your index finger. In stubborn cases, you can roll the leaf and fasten it with Scotch tape. When you remove the tape, the leaf will spring back into a curved direction. Stiff materials like palm spathe, pods, and bark become pliable by soaking them in very hot water. In cases where the material is extremely stiff, you can even boil it.

Foliage arrangements are satisfactory for several reasons. In the first place, they are extremely long-lasting. They are lovely in them-

Arrangement by Mrs. Harold Brooks

Figure 10. This large mass arrangement is made primarily with foliage that grows in many dooryards. Ilex, andromeda, and leucothoe are used with an accent of white narcissus. The flowers could be omitted, and just the foliage used, with the andromeda clusters grouped at the focal point. (Photo by Roche)

selves, but can also form a background arrangement for the addition of a few flowers. The arrangement in Fig. 10 is such an arrangement. It would be charming without any flowers at all, but it is such that without changing the foliage you can have a variety of arrangements by using different flowers. Much material is easily available for a mass arrangement such as this, or you can have a simple but eye-compelling arrangement with three beautifully curved large leaves.

Foliage arrangements are a good choice for contemporary or modern houses. The bold clean-cut lines of the simple arrangements make an attractive silhouette against the expanse of plain walls, and blend with the streamlined furnishings. Mass arrangements of foliage can be placed against the glass walls of such houses, and not only look well on each side of the glass, but serve as a good transition between the room and the landscape outside.

As brilliant colors usually surround the outside of the Spanish-type houses of the South and West, it is restful and cool to use arrangements inside in all the shades and color intensities of green.

During the hot spells that come in summer, even in the northern part of the country, it would be refreshing to see the opening of the fireplace filled with masses of rhododendron, laurel, or fern, and on a cold autumn day a simulated fire of red and gold leaves. When you use autumn leaves it is a good idea to take a lesson from Nature. Just as the scarlet and yellow of maples and the gold of hickories on the hillsides seem more brilliant because they are interspersed among the dark green of evergreens, arrangements using these leaves are more effective when they are combined with some dark green foliage.

Because leaves and branches are so typical of the out-of-doors, naturalistic containers are especially suited to them. Interesting pieces of driftwood, lichen-covered tree stumps, or a weathered root are suitable. Foliage arrangements, using a cup pinholder, can be made on a flat rock, a burl, or a piece of polished wood. More conventional containers can be used, too. Those of wood, like a bowl, a mortar, or a square pillow vase are all good. I recently saw an unusual one that had been made by winding twine closely around a fruit juice can, and then shellacking it. Oriental containers give great distinction to foliage arrangements.

An object is often used as an accessory with a foliage arrangement, either to complete the outdoor mood, or continue the line of the design. For instance the figure of a squirrel, properly placed at the base of an arrangement of leafed branches, would suggest the woods. Or the curved wings or neck of a duck might be the touch needed to complete a curved line in an arrangement. You might use an unusual rock at the base to give visual weight and stability to soaring branches. Whatever you choose, be sure that it blends with the arrangement in scale, color, and texture, so that it seems an integral part of the whole.

Following is a list of foliage that is suitable for arrangements, with a brief description. It would be well worth growing some of the ones that are labeled as houseplants, or suitable for dooryard planting, in order to have material readily available for arrangements.

FOLIAGE USEFUL FOR ARRANGEMENTS

Name	*Description*	*Where Found*
Andromeda (an-*drom*eda)	Evergreen. Clusters of leaves that are bronze, red, or chartreuse depending on season. Irregular.	Widely grown shrub. Suitable for dooryard planting.
Artemisia (ar-teh-*mee*-see-a)	Gray- or ivory-colored. Soft feathery spikes.	Gardens. Florist.
Aspidistra (ass-pi-*dis*-tra)	Long wide leaf, one to two feet long, tapered at end. Rich green. Spiky.	Easily grown houseplant, or obtainable at florist's.
Azalea (a-*zay*-lee-a)	Clusters of tiny shiny dark green leaves on stiff stem. Turns red in autumn. Irregular.	Widely grown shrub. Suitable for dooryard planting.
Beech	Copper- or purple-colored oval leaves of large tree widely grown in United States. Graceful branches.	

Name	Description	Where Found
Begonia (bee-*go*-nee-a), many varieties	Leaves of many shapes depending on variety. Good for use at focal point.	Grown as houseplant. Obtainable at florist's.
Billbergia (bill-*burr*-gee-a)	Blue-green rigid pineapplelike leaves. Spiky.	Obtainable at florist's.
Caladium (cal-*ade*-ee-um)	Large heart-shaped leaves. Red and green, white and green, white with red. Irregular.	Grown in tropical climates. Obtainable at florist's.
Calla	Large leathery arrow-shaped leaves. Spiky.	Grows in warm climates. At florist's.
Camellia (ka-*meal*-ee-a)	Dark shiny green leaves alternating on stem. Sturdy stem. Spiky.	Grown outdoors in South and West. Obtainable at florist's.
Canna	Long, wide tapering leaves, tinged with red or violet. Spiky.	Widely grown outdoors in United States.
Carnation	Feathery blue-green spirals from sheath. Spiky.	Grows in warm climates. At florist's.
Catbrier	Like large-leafed smilax. Vine.	Grows wild in many states.
Cedrus atlantica (*seed*-rus at-*lan*-tee-ka), or Atlantic Cedar	Evergreen tree. Blue-green needles in tiny rosettes along branch. Especially desirable. Spiky.	Grows Northeast. Some florist's.
Clematis (*klem*-ah-tis)	Green. Climbing plant. Grows in beautiful curves. Good for line arrangements, or to add interesting curves.	Grows outdoors except far North.
Coleus (*ko*-lee-us)	Pointed leaves alternating on short stem, ending in cluster. Yellow, chartreuse, pink, red, purple, variegated. Irregular.	Grows in gardens or as houseplant.

Name	*Description*	*Where Found*
Croton (*kro*-ton)	Long narrow leaves from 4 to 18 inches. Others broad, some spiral. Brilliant colors —pink, red, crimson, yellow, orange, variegated. Spiky.	Grows outdoors in tropics and semitropics. At florist's.
Cyclamen (*sigh*-cla-men)	Small heart-shaped leaves. Green. Marked and veined with lighter green. Round.	Houseplant.
Dieffenbachia (deef-en-*bock*-ia)	Large wide tapered leaves. Green, spotted or veined with white. Individual leaves used in arrangement. Spiky.	Grown in tropical climates. Houseplant. At florist's.
Dracaena (drah-*see*-na)	Large wide curved leaves. Green and yellow, green and white. Spiky.	Outdoors in warm climates. At florist's. Houseplant.
Eucalyptus (you-ka-*lip*-tus)	Gray-blue-green leaves, small and round, grow in spiral on long stem. Spiky.	Trees in tropical and semitropical climates. At florist's.
Euonymous (you-*on*-ee-muss)	Small leaves grow closely on leathery stem. Grows as bush or vine. Glossy green, silver-edged. Gold, gold and green. Spiky.	Evergreen. Grows outdoors many states. Suitable for dooryard planting.
Euphorbia (you-*for*-bee-a), or Snow-on-the-Mountain	Low growing. Small green leaves edged with white, grow in flowerlike clusters. Irregular.	Widely grown in gardens.
Ferns, many varieties	Many shapes depending on variety. Feathery. Lacy. Irregular.	Grow wild in woods, or as houseplants.
Galax (*gay*-lax)	Large heart-shaped leaves. Leathery texture. Stiff short stem. Round.	Grows in eastern North America.

Name	*Description*	*Where Found*
Geranium	Ruffly velvety green leaves. Round.	Grows outdoors widely. Houseplant.
Hickory	Leaves of forest tree golden in autumn. Branches.	Native American tree.
Holly	Dark green, or green and white glossy spiny leaves and red berries grow along woody stem. Branches.	Grows widely in United States. Obtainable at florist's.
Hosta, or Funkia	Blue-green, green, or green and white. Some varieties have large grooved heart-shaped leaves. Others long, curved, pointed. Individual leaves used.	Widely grown in gardens.
Huckleberry	Flat dark green leaves growing flat on woody stem. Spiky.	Grows wild in many parts of North America. At florist's.
Ilex (*eye*-lex)	Tiny smooth dark green leaves growing densely on stem. Evergreen. Small branches.	Suitable for dooryard planting.
Ivy	Climbing plant. Five-pointed leaf. Graceful sprays. Single leaf used as irregular form.	Grows widely out of doors or as houseplant.
Ivy Geranium	Plant grows in cascading form. Leaf shaped like ivy. Irregular.	Grows outdoors in warm climate or as houseplant.
Juniper	Evergreen. Feathery gray-green. Slate blue berries grow on stem. Some varieties turn bronze in fall. Spiky.	Suitable for dooryard plantings or landscaping.

Name	*Description*	*Where Found*
Laurel (lah-rell)	Evergreen shrub. Oval pointed leaves grow in clusters on stiff stem. Branches. Clusters good in fruit arrangements.	Suitable for dooryard planting. As cut foliage at florist's. Grows wild in many parts of country.
Leucothoe (lew-*ko*-tho-ee)	Evergreen. Pointed leaves alternating on wandlike stem. Leathery texture. Colors change at different seasons from green to purplish green, bronze, and chartreuse. Spiky.	Grows widely. Suitable for dooryard planting.
Loquat (*low*-kwat)	Small evergreen shrub tree. Strong dark green leaves growing on branch. Spiky.	Grows in semitropics.
Magnolia	Many varieties. Large green oval leaves on branch. Some have brown on underside. Good for preserving with glycerin. Used as branches or individual leaves.	Widely grown in Southern United States. At florist's.
Mahonia (mah-*hoe*-nee-a)	Low-growing evergreen shrub with green or bronze hollylike leaf.	Suitable for dooryard planting.
Maple	Leaves grow on branches of native forest tree. In fall various colors of red, yellow, and orange.	Grows widely.
Oak	Leaves on branches of native forest tree. Red or brown in autumn. Branches.	Grows widely. At florist's.
Pachysandra (pack-i-*san*-dra)	Green serrated leaves grow in rosettes on soft stem. Good to use at focal point or in fruit arrangements.	Widely grown as ground cover.

Name	Description	Where Found
Pandanus (pan-*day*-nus)	Swordlike leaves two to three feet long. Green with yellow or white stripes. Spiky.	Grows in warm climates or as houseplant. At florist's.
Philodendron (fill-oh-*den*-dron)	Many varieties and shapes. Graceful sprays, or interesting single leaves. Useful at focal point.	Grows in warm climates. Houseplants.
Pine, many varieties	Evergreen needled branches.	Grows widely.
Pittosporum (pitt-*us*-pore-um)	Evergreen. Thick oval leaves grow in flowerlike cluster. Branches or clusters used at focal point.	Grows in mild climates. At florist's.
Podocarpus (poe-doe-*car*-puss)	Evergreen. Dark green featherlike plumes. Can be bent to graceful curves. Spiky.	Grows to small tree in warm climates. At florist's.
Privet	Small semi-evergreen leaves grow along woody stem. Some varieties yellow. Spiky.	Grows widely in bushes and hedges.
Rhododendron (roe-doe-*den*-drun)	Dark green evergreen shrub. Long oval leaves growing in circle around branch. Good for large mass arrangements.	Widely grown. Grows wild in many states. Suitable for dooryard planting.
Sansevieria (san-see-*veer*-e-a)	Thick, green sword-shaped leaf one to two feet long. Some striped and marked with yellow. Spiky.	Grows outdoors in semitropics. Houseplant.
Scotch Broom	Thin, stringlike strands growing in plumes. Dark green. Easily shaped in curves. Spiky.	Grows widely as outdoor bush. At florist's.

Name	*Description*	*Where Found*
Sea Grape	Large round leathery green leaves. Some tinged with red or bronze. Used as single leaves. Round.	Grows wild in southern part of country.
Ti	Long narrow tapering leaves. Green, with red-violet tinge.	Tropical. Obtainable at florist's.
Violet	Small heart-shaped green leaves. Round.	Grows wild and in gardens.
Yew	Very dark green evergreen shrub. Small needles an inch long grow flat on branches. Spiky.	Suitable for dooryard planting.

ARRANGEMENTS OF
FLOWERING TREES,
SHRUBS, AND VINES

MOST people think of garden flowers, those purchased from a florist, or wildflowers when they think of arrangements. But some of the loveliest are those of flowering shrubs, climbing vines, and fruit and forest trees.

One woman that I know has recently done a very clever thing. In her eighties, and suffering from arthritis, she has had her lovely garden changed from one of annuals and perennials to a garden of shrubs, vines, and flowering trees. "You know," she said, "I have always loved wandering around the garden and getting inspiration for my arrangements by cutting things when I see them growing. It isn't at all the same when plant material is brought to you already cut. So, since I can no longer stoop over, I am having my flowers at a level where I don't have to bend."

As a result, she has a cutting garden from earliest spring, when she can force flowering branches, until late in the fall and winter, when some of the berries are loveliest. And among these things there is a wealth of flower forms to make interesting arrangements.

If you want to be like my elderly friend, and have a garden of flowering shrubs, trees, and vines, here are some that will give you beautiful arrangement material.

SHRUBS

Abelia	Handsome semi-evergreen small-leafed foliage. Small tubular flowers in white, pink, or rose that bloom all summer. When flowers drop in fall, attractive clusters of dusty pink bracts are left. Grows in mild climates as far north as southern New England.
Bridal Wreath, or Spiraea	Round clusters of tiny white flowers all along arching stems. Blooms in spring.
Butterfly Bush, or Buddleia	Spikes of lavender and purple flowers that are fragrant and bloom in the summer. Given its common name because it attracts butterflies.
Camellia	Glossy green leaves and showy large single, semidouble and double flowers of white and many shades of pink and red. Grows mostly in South and West, but with protection will grow as far north as New Jersey.
Ceanothus	Lovely clusters of flowers in shades of blue. Grows in Pacific coast area. A collection of different varieties will give bloom from spring until fall.
Cotoneaster	Very interesting for attractive growth of branches and colorful berries in fall. Small leaves turn a lovely red in fall. Grows in temperate regions and hardy quite far north.
Fire Thorn, or Pyracantha	The clusters of small white flowers that appear in summer are insignificant, but are followed in the fall by gorgeous orange-red berries that last most of the winter.
Flowering Almond, or Prunus	Stems covered with small pink and white blossoms resembling button chrysanthemum. Blooms in early spring.

Forsythia

Deep yellow bell-shaped flowers circle wand-like stems in March and April. Leaves appear after flowers drop. Grows in Northeast.

Hibiscus

Interesting for large trumpet-shaped pink, scarlet, yellow, apricot, crimson flowers that bloom in spring, summer, and fall in warm climates. Flower heads will last for a day out of water.

Hydrangea

Very large flower heads of cream, pink, or blue. Flowers last all summer and in fall turn to shades of lavender, blue green, green, and bronze.

Japanese Quince, or Chaenomeles Lagenaria

Blooms in early spring with lovely blossoms resembling tiny wild roses. Flowers are light pink when forced. Otherwise rose red. Lustrous green leaves appear after flowers. Grows in Northeast. Small fruits not edible but give delightful fragrance to bureau drawers.

Lilac

Flower heads are large terminal bushy pyramids of florets in many shades—lavender, purple, pinky lavender, white, and lavender blue. They are very fragrant. They bloom in spring and early summer in the Northeast.

Mock Orange, or Philadelphus

This shrub probably got its common name because its fragrance is similar to that of orange blossoms. It is sometimes mistakenly called Syringa. The small satiny white flowers, with prominent orange stamens, grow on pliant branches. It blooms in June in the Northeast.

Snowberry, or Symphoricarpos

Attractive for its clusters of globular waxy white berries in the fall, which last for several months. Grows widely.

Stewartia	Has large white or cream-colored flowers like single roses, which bloom all summer along the Atlantic coast. An outstanding shrub not commonly planted.
Vitex	Grows outdoors in warm climates and as far north as southern New England. Has slender spiky lilac-colored terminal flower heads. Blooms in late August and September.

FLOWERING VINES

Bittersweet	Vigorous hardy climbing vines, suitable for walls and fences. Valued for arrangements for the yellow berries which pop open in the autumn to expose bright red seeds inside. Also grows wild, but should not be picked then as it is on conservation lists.
Clematis	This grows in temperate regions, and is suitable for fences, trellises, or walls. There are many kinds and it is possible to have a succession of bloom from spring to fall. According to variety the flowers are small or large. Many are fragrant. There are many colors—white, blue, lilac, rose, pink, yellow, and purple. The vines have tendrils that are graceful for arrangements.
Cup-and-Saucer, or Cobaea	The common name is suggested by the large violet bell-shaped flowers with a large leafy calyx at the base. This is a good climber. In arrangements the flower is distinctive, as is the dried calyx. Blooms in summer.
Dutchman's-Pipe, or Aristolochia	This vine grows in warm climates. Has large heart-shaped leaves, and pipe-shaped flowers from which it gets its common name. It blooms in June and July. Its value to the arranger is the unusually shaped flower,

83

	and the seed pod which comes in the fall, like a fluted parachute that hasn't quite opened.
Passionflower, or Passiflora	This vine grows in warm climates, or indoors in the North. Has wide flat flowers in a mixture of blue, lavender and white, pink and red. The flowers, thought by many to be emblematic of the crucifixion of Christ, are striking, and the vines grow in fascinating tendrils.
Trumpet Vine, or Campsis	A strong climber, this vine has feathery leaves and funnel-shaped flowers of orange and red. Blooms in August and September.

When you select flowering branches, look for ones that are growing at interesting angles. By judicious pruning, you can emphasize these. You will need a heavy pinholder, and the pins must be sharp. If you make little crisscross cuts on the end of the branch, you can spread it into a brush and have a larger surface to stick on the pins. If you want the branches at an angle, it is better to jam it firmly on the pinholder in a vertical position and then push it to the slant you want, rather than try and impale it on the pinholder at an angle. If you use a tall container, of course a pinholder isn't necessary.

Flowering branches are lovely arranged by themselves. You might put Japanese quince in a tall black tea caddy. Its dull black color is a dramatic contrast with the pale salmon pink flowers. Apricot branches, with their black bark and stark white flowers seem to call for a white pottery container. A low Persian copper plate is a good choice for branches of star magnolia, whose long pointed brown buds are so attractive, while pussy willows seem a natural for pewter.

If you want to use other flowers with branches, why not take a lesson from the Japanese and use flowers that would naturally be growing with them? Violets, crocuses, or grape hyacinths can be arranged at the base so that they look as though they were growing naturally under a blossoming tree. Tulips, daffodils, and narcissus seem just right to use with them. If you use the leaves of these flowering bulbs, instead of inserting them individually, try nesting several leaves of different lengths together and bind the bottom with Scotch tape. Then insert them as one into a pinholder. For a leaf to bend, curl it around your index finger, pressing it softly as you do it.

In houses of contemporary style, driftwood or gnarled tree stumps make distinctive containers for flowering branches. You can use a cup pinholder that holds water and hide it behind the wood. Or if you have a stump or piece of driftwood that you will use often, you can hollow out a place for the pinholder to fit, and fasten it there permanently.

Some of the most beautiful flowers available for arrangements are those of large trees that are known mostly for their foliage. Because these are often very high, the blossoms sometimes go unnoticed. These flowers are doubly precious, because they are

Arrangement by
Catherine H. Smith

Figure 11. Chartreuse Norway maple blossoms and daffodils are combined to make an arrangement that is the essence of spring. Note how the placement of the daffodils gives interest and dimension to the design. (Photo by Roche)

85

available for such a short season. One of the most beautiful is the flower of the tulip tree (liriodendron). This tree is common in the forests of the Eastern seaboard, and in late May and early June has an exquisite six-petaled cup-shaped blossom. The petals are chartreuse green, with a yellow-bordered salmony orange center. I saw a woman look at an arrangement of these once at a flower show, and heard her say, "What do you suppose those exotic flowers are? They must have come from the tropics." I laughed to myself, because I knew that half an hour earlier she had walked under a row of tulip trees in bloom on the golf course.

Another of my favorites is the blossom of the Norway maple— a tree that lines so many of our suburban streets, parkways, and highways. In the spring the flower is a spray like a miniature sky-rocket of tiny pale yellow stars. Perhaps they are used more as cut flowers because people looking casually mistake them for early foliage. But they *are* flowers, harden well, and are beautiful in arrangements, as is shown in Fig. 11.

Many admire the tall pink or white candles of the horsechestnut tree but, perhaps because they grow so high, don't think to pick them. These are well worth getting a ladder and climbing for, because they also harden well (pound the stem ends) and make most striking arrangements.

These are but a few examples of many of the flowers you will find on trees if you will keep your "seeing eye" open.

FLOWERING TREES

Dogwood

This is found from Massachusetts to Florida. It is wonderful for arrangements in the spring, when it is white with what are mistakenly called flowers but are really waxy white bracts surrounding small green flower heads. These appear before the leaves, and grow on flat branches. In the fall the berries are scarlet and the foliage is gorgeous with many shades of red or green. Although it is among the most beautiful of plants for arrangements during the year, it is on the conservation list in many states, and should not be picked where it is growing wild. Fortunately it is becoming one of the most popular cultivated trees.

Fruit Trees

Almost all fruit trees have beautiful blossoms in the spring. Some, in addition to bearing edible fruit, have varieties that are grown for their ornamental blossoms, like some cherry and crab apple trees.

Horsechestnut

Grows widely over the United States. It has handsome upright stalks of flowers like huge candles. This is an impressive flower that is seen too seldom in flower arrangements. Mostly white or pink, but some varieties may be yellow, purple, or red.

Mountain Ash

This tree grows in the northern part of the United States, and has sprays of white flowers in the spring, and clusters of orange-red berries in the fall. It is the berries, rather than the flowers, that are valuable for arrangements.

Norway Maple

This tree is common to most of the country. In the spring it has showering sprays of tiny chartreuse flowers.

Redbud Tree, or Cercis

This tree, sometimes called Judas Tree, grows over most of temperate North America. It has red buds in winter, and in the spring, before the leaves appear, clusters of purple-rose flowers shaped like tiny sweet peas.

Star Magnolia, or Magnolia Stellata

This is a small tree with angular branches, and is spectacular for white starlike flowers and long pointed buds which appear before the leaves. Grows widely.

ARRANGEMENTS OF FORCED
BRANCHES AND FLOWERING SHRUBS

IN PARTS of the country where winter snow and cold make you long for spring, it is fun to cut branches of flowering shrubs, fruit trees, or other trees and bring them inside the house where they will be forced into bloom. It is thrilling to be able in this way to extend their naturally short blooming time.

About the earliest that you can force them successfully is late January or early February. It will take from one to several weeks, depending upon how close to the natural blooming time you cut them. However, if you cut branches that are interesting in shape, you can enjoy the linear pattern even before the buds begin to swell and the leaves and blossoms appear. Don't cut so many that the charm of the individual branch is lost.

On one of the mild days that are apt to come in the middle of winter, go out and see what you can find. You may take something from your dooryard like laurel, rhododendron, andromeda, azalea, star magnolia, or something from the garden like forsythia, bridal wreath, syringa, lilac, or Japanese quince. The latter, incidentally, whose normal color is a little harsh for some people's taste, is a delicate soft pink when forced. In your yard you may get dogwood, Japanese maple, beech, birch, or horsechestnut. On a walk in the country keep your eyes open for pussy willow, swamp maple, witch hazel, spice bush, or alder. Fruit trees—apple, pear, cherry, apricot, plum, and crab apple—are all wonderful for forcing. The leaves and flowers have a delicacy in form and color that is enchanting.

Cut branches of a generous length, just above a strong bud. Use a sharp knife or pruning shears. Select ones that are of a medium thickness, and avoid ones that are twiggy. After you have cut them, pound the ends of the stems with a hammer, or slit them and peel the bark back a little, so that they will absorb a maximum amount of water. If you cut the branches very early in the season, put them in the bathtub and cover them with tepid water overnight. While they are forcing, put them in a deep container of water in a room with a temperature of 65 to 70 degrees. Your living room will probably be fine, and they are so decorative that you will want them where you can see them often. For this reason I always keep some in the kitchen. Change the water frequently. As moisture helps the buds and flowers develop, spray them from time to time.

You can bring a corner of your garden into the house weeks ahead of time with an arrangement of forsythia and daffodils. Purple violets with pussy willows will make you long for a spring wildflower pilgrimage. And the tiny forced leaves of sweet gum branches combined with the first curved shoots of skunk cabbage will make you forget the March winds howling outside.

FRUIT ARRANGEMENTS

I T USED to be that a "fruit arrangement" meant a heaping bowl of bananas, oranges, apples, and grapes placed on a sideboard or dining room table. Each member of the family who passed usually helped himself to a tempting bit until before long the arrangement was pretty dilapidated.

Fruits and vegetables are such decorative plant material that it seems a pity not to use them just for that purpose. By all means have the family fruit bowl, but relegate it to the pantry, where the family can nibble to its heart's content. Design another as part of your decorative scheme—and not just for the dining room, either. Fruits and vegetables come in such a wide variety of color and form that you aren't limited to conventional arrangements. The possibilities for using them in entrance halls, living rooms, kitchen, and study are endless.

Bananas, pineapples, eggplant, and long-necked squash give height to an arrangement. Apples, oranges, plums, limes, tangerines, peaches, and pomegranates are basic round forms. Pears, avocados, nectarines, persimmons, and plum tomatoes lend interest with their triangular and elliptical shapes. And grapes, bananas, peppers, and gourds are curved. You will find it interesting to combine these forms.

As for color, there is every color imaginable. Pineapples are not always brown and green—they also come in orange and rosy tints. Pears can be brown, green, pink, or blush red. Plums are green, flame, yellow, red, and purple. Apples are green, yellow, red, and red-violet. You can certainly make an arrangement in almost any color scheme you wish.

To give your fruit arrangements distinction, learn to use material that is a little unusual. In the late spring tiny pineapples, only three or four inches long, with plumy green tops come on the market. These are too small to sell in food markets but are available through a florist and are charming to use. Pokeberry weed, which gives distinction to an arrangement with its clusters of purplish black berries on red stems, is to be had for the picking —but when you do pick it, take a cigarette lighter with you to sear the stems. Often, when a stem of bananas is delivered to a fruit market, there is a group of tiny undeveloped bananas at the top. These the dealer cuts off and throws away, and they aren't seen by the general public. If you ask your dealer to save them for you, you will be delighted when you see what fun they are to use.

Osage oranges, the yellowish green fruit of the maclura tree, add lovely color and interesting texture to an arrangement. Try using kumquats in branches rather than singly. And if you know anyone who has a mandarin orange tree, beg, borrow, or steal some of the smallest. They are like tiny tangerines, only an inch in diameter.

When you go to a market to select fruit for an arrangement, don't feel that you have to buy it by the pound. If you only want one of this, or two of that, put them in separate bags and have them weighed individually.

Foliage with a leathery texture is good to use in fruit arrangements. It holds up better than some of the more delicate types, and usually has glossy leaves which are in harmony with the gloss of the fruit. Clusters of laurel will last well without being in water. To put them in an arrangement, hold the three or four leaves of the cluster tightly together with your thumb and first two fingers, and insert the stem into a space between pieces of fruit. When you release them, the leaves will expand in a natural-looking way.

Leucothoe, green in summer and purply bronze in winter, is another excellent foliage for fruit arrangements. Andromeda clusters, with fascinating showers of flowers like tiny pearls, are interesting. Bold leaves like canna, sansevieria, aspidistra, and magnolia help in forming a design.

For foliage in fruit arrangements that needs to be in water, you can use water picks. You can either stick the picks in a pinholder, or wedge them among the fruit. Conceal them, of course.

You are not limited to the conventional bowl or compote as a container. You could use a bread tray, a brass lamp base, scales, graduated boards like steps, footed bowls, silver cake baskets and even bamboo mats.

It goes without saying that all fruit, vegetables, and foliage should be without blemishes, and sparkling clean. The best way to clean them is to rub them with waxed paper.

Making fruit and vegetables is rather like playing blocks. You start with a firm foundation, and then each piece rests against the other, and they are mutually dependent for balance and support. Just as with flower arranging, there are ways to use mechanical aids to make the different pieces stay where you want them. You will need scissors, pinholders, clay, florist's picks, toothpicks and water picks. And just as with a flower arrangement, you must have a design or pattern in mind before you start working.

To see how to go about making a fruit arrangement, let's make

a hypothetical one in a Hogarth, or S curve, on a large flat compote, using fruits in the pink to purple range.

The first thing to do after deciding on the design and color combination is to select the piece of fruit that will be the physical foundation of the arrangement. This is usually the one that gives height also. The next step is to plan the mechanics so that this piece of fruit or vegetable will be *absolutely* firm, for it will be the foundation stone for the whole arrangement.

For this arrangement, we will choose a large tapered eggplant, selecting one that has a curved green stem that will indicate the top of the S curve of the design. Fasten a good-sized needleholder on the compote with Stickum, so that it is secure. This should be placed a little left of center, as shown in the drawing on page 92. Impale the eggplant firmly on it, as indicated by the top of the S. The design will curve from the tip of the green stem of the eggplant, which should be above the center of the arrangement.

Now choose several small rosy apples of uniform size, and place them flat side down on the compote at the base of the eggplant, anchoring them on the pins at the edge of the pinholder. These will mostly be covered later by other fruit, but will form a base for the center of the design.

To make the bottom curve of the S, we will use rose-colored Tokay grapes. As the eggplant curved to the left of center, these will curve to the right. In selecting grapes for a fruit arrangement, it is not necessary to find a perfectly shaped bunch in the store. It is often better to make your own by wiring pieces of bunches together to make just the shape you want. In this case, we want the bunch to hang over the edge of the compote, curving to the right, and then reversing to the left at the tip to finish the S curve which started with the tip of the eggplant stem.

So, selecting a small bunch with a sturdy stem end, we will wire two or three clusters to it in such a way that it will have the desired curve. Now take a florist's pick, and wire it firmly to the stem end of the bunch, and thrust the other end deep into one of the foundation apples at the base of the eggplant. In this way the grapes are anchored and will hang freely without falling. We now have the skeleton of an S curve design.

Make a focal point by placing a dark red apple in the center of the S curve, with the blossom end facing out for added interest. Now we fill in with fruits, always keeping in mind the S design. To support the line made by the eggplant, choose a green pear with a curvy stem and place it on one of the foundation apples, leaning against the left side of the eggplant, with its stem curving in the same direction as the eggplant stem. This emphasizes the top curve. To make sure it won't fall off, break a florist's pick in half, remove the wire, and put one of the short sticks in the bottom of the pear. Then thrust the other end of the stick into the apple on which the pear will rest. Now it will stay put. If you were unable to find a pear which had a rosy tint on the green (which would be a nice transitional color in the arrangement) take your lipstick and rub a little on the pear. Then, with your thumb rub it well into the skin and I defy anyone to detect it from Nature's own coloring.

On the other side of the eggplant, toward the center, you could put a small green avocado. Its dark color makes a good contrast, and its tip tapering toward the eggplant also strengthens the line of the design. With other small apples, plums, and limes, build fruits up toward the eggplant and down toward the grapes. Keep darker colors toward the center. Fasten them to each other with sticks if necessary to keep them from tumbling. The arrangement doesn't take a quantity of fruit, but each piece must be placed as a definite part of the design.

Finally, take a small bunch of dark purple grapes which will be draped at the focal point to emphasize it. These will lie on top of the fruit, and so that there will be a flat side to enable them to do this, hold the bunch in your hand, and snip off the grapes on the under side. Then spread the bunch, and put it flat side down on the fruit at the focal point, draping it around it. Now take little clusters of Tokay grapes and place them over the other fruit so that there will be a flowing line of grapes from the eggplant to the tip of the overhanging bunch at the bottom. When the front of the arrangement suits you, turn it around, and put some fruit where it may be needed to complete the back of the design. Then tuck some clusters of leaves in spaces between the fruit. The arrangement in Plate 6 was done in this way.

If you are making an arrangement and you want the effect of a bunch of grapes and you don't have any, you can use cranberries, strawberries, blackberries, cherries, or nuts. Fasten cranberries, strawberries, or blackberries with toothpicks to the fruit below, in the form of clusters. Wire clusters of cherries together to make a bunch. Drill small holes through the tops of nuts, put wire through them, and wire them into bunches

Fruit arrangements are excellent to use as centerpieces for a buffet table. When the table is against a wall, you can use bold leaves for the background design. For an arrangement in shades of violet and red you could use canna or ti leaves with eggplant, red and purple plums, red and purple grapes, and pokeberry arranged on a jagged piece of gray flagstone.

Or, you might have an arrangement in shades of yellow and brown, using glycerined brown magnolia leaves with a brown pineapple, bananas, brown-skinned onions, lemons, and yellow apples on a bamboo mat.

Autumn berries are attractive used in combination with fruits and vegetables. Imagine brilliant orange fire thorn berries used with orange-streaked green peppers, or turquoise beauty berries with purple plums and grapes.

It is great fun, though, to use fruit arrangements in rooms other than dining rooms. A pineapple is a symbol of hospitality. What better place for a fruit arrangement featuring a pineapple than on a hall table where it would be a welcoming note for guests. You could make an unusual one, using the tiny pineapples we mentioned. Their lush green tops have wonderful curves. You could make a line mass arrangement using just the pineapples. You might use a footed globular brass jardiniere. Put a block of Oasis into it vertically, so that about four inches is above the rim. Impale the pineapples on sticks of varying lengths, and stick them into the Oasis at various angles, so that the green tops form the line of the design.

Some Victorian houses are austere and cold, but I know of one that is full of warmth. The woman who owns it usually has a fruit arrangement in her living room, where the colors of the glowing coals in a Victorian iron grate are repeated on a nearby table by polished dark red apples, purple plums, and red and purple grapes piled in an iron stove top. A further tie to the fire is given by pieces of red coleus fringed with yellow which are snipped from her houseplants, placed in water picks, and inserted into the fruit arrangement.

With their bold forms and smooth textures, fruits and vegetables are ideal for decoration in houses of modern and contempo-

Arrangement by Katherine N. Cutler

Figure 12. A fruit arrangement in shades of yellow, brown, and green. Hawthorn with its haws, lemons, limes, green grapes, and brown pears are arranged in a brass estribo (South American stirrup) placed on a mahogany board. Note crescent design from top branch, through curved groove in estribo, to stem of farthest pear. This arrangement could be used in a living room on a desk, mantel, or side table. (Photo by Roche)

rary design. An upright fan of green bananas, placed at the top of graduated black boards, accented by slender curving green peppers, combined with scarlet plum tomatoes and chunks of green glass slag would be attractive in such a house.

I don't think you would ordinarily think of a dark green glass gallon bottle as a container for a fruit arrangement, and yet I saw one used for an arrangement in a contemporary house that was dramatic. The bottle was placed on two rectangular dark green boards, one slightly larger than the other. The arrangement was a vertical design, with curved yellow striped sansevieria leaves making the top lines. These were inserted into the neck of the bottle. The tall main line was emphasized by a branch of kumquats. The focal point at the neck was formed with clusters of yellow and green variegated euonymous, and a few small lemons (impaled on sticks stuck into the neck of the bottle). More kumquats spilled down the bottle toward an arrangement of fruit on the boards at the base of the bottle. This was formed of an avocado, lemons, limes, tiny bananas, and kumquats.

The arrangement in Fig. 12 was designed for the top of a desk in an Early American house, but actually it would fit into almost any period of decoration. The container is a brass estribo—an antique South American stirrup—placed on a mahogany board. The design, following the grooved curves in the estribo, is a modified crescent, using hawthorn with its haws, lemons, limes, green grapes, and brown pears.

Kitchen arrangements are fun, too. Instead of putting green fruit along a window sill to ripen, did you ever think of making an arrangement with it? Some green tomatoes, a hard avocado, and some unripened plums, with the addition of a handful of parsley or sprigs of mint (in water picks) could be an attractive kitchen arrangement that you could enjoy while you are waiting to eat it.

ARRANGEMENTS OF DRIED MATERIAL

Hanging HAVE you ever stood in your garden on a June day looking at a partly opened rose, or an intensely blue delphinium, and thought, "Oh, if I could only save it"? You can, by drying it. You can preserve that very rose and use it in an arrangement in January when its parent bush is covered with snow.

Many people, when they think of dried arrangements, think only of those made from material which has dried naturally, like seed pods, pine cones, fungus, and dead branches. These, in neutral shades of brown and gray are fascinating and desirable. But you can also have dried arrangements that are bursting with color, like the ones in Plates 4 and 12. Best of all, they can be the very flowers you have carefully tended in your garden. There are several ways to dry flowers, and the method depends on the type of flower.

The first is known as Hanging. This method is very easy, and is best for sturdy flowers like cockscomb, goldenrod, bittersweet, euphorbia, yarrow, etc. Pick the flowers just before they reach their prime (an exception is hydrangea, which should be left on the bush until it is a little past the height of its bloom). Strip off any leaves. Tie the flowers in small bunches and hang them head down in a dry place with very little light, such as a dark attic, or a closet. Darkness preserves the color. Unless it is a heated furnace room, don't use a cellar, as it is apt to be damp. It will take from two to four weeks for the flowers to dry.

Another method of drying single flowers, or delicate flowers *Drying* that grow on a stalk, is by using a drying mixture. Some people *Mixture* like to use a mixture of two-thirds borax and one-third construction sand. I happen to like to use plain sand. It takes longer for the flowers to dry, but I think they have a better color than with the borax combination.

I use beach sand, which is of excellent consistency, but which contains salt that must be removed. To do this, you can fill a large preserving kettle two-thirds full of sand, and add water to the brim. Stir the sand around and around in the water, then pour off the water, repeating this process seven times. Then spread it on a newspaper to dry. If beach sand isn't available, you can buy the kind used for children's sand boxes at a lumber yard.

The drying mixture method is excellent for flowers like daisies, dahlias, roses, daffodils, carnations, pinks, Queen Anne's lace, foxgloves, petunias, dogwood, snapdragons, gladiolus, delphiniums, lilies, gaillardias, veronicas, coralbells, cosmos, pansies, and coreopsis.

Pick the flowers before they have quite reached full bloom, at a time when there hasn't been a recent rain, and when they are not covered with dew. In other words, they should be as dry as possible when you start. Remember, too, that the more moisture a flower retains naturally in its petals, like a lily, the longer it will take to dry.

Remove the stem of the flower, as it is very brittle and hard to handle when dry, and stick a short wire through the flower at the place where the stem joins it, pulling the ends down and twisting them together. (After the flower is dry, you can add another wire of any desired length to this short wire, and cover it with green floral tape so that it looks like a natural stem. You can bend this "stem" any way you want it in an arrangement.)

It is fun to experiment drying with sand. There is no set list of which flowers will be successful because you more or less have to do it by trial. Don't be afraid to try any since you have nothing to lose, and a thrill in store if it turns out well.

Put an inch of sand (or whatever drying mixture you are using) on the bottom of a strong box like a shoe box, and put the flower with the wire bent so that it will lie flat, face up on the sand. Supporting the flower petals with your left hand to hold them in

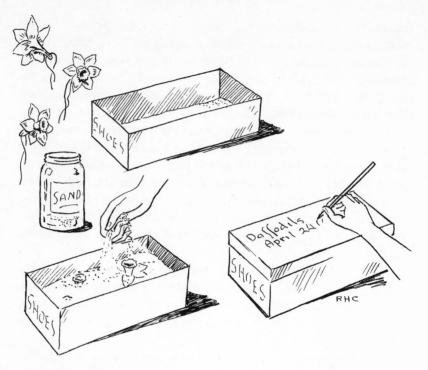

position, sift the mixture gently over, around, and through the petals of the flower until it is entirely buried. Repeat this until the surface of the sand is covered, but be sure the flowers don't touch each other. Then put a lid on the box and mark it as to date and contents.

With plain sand, it will take the flowers from one to three weeks to dry. With borax they dry from a few days to a week. As no two flowers are alike in their drying time you have to experiment a little. Daisies dry quickly, roses and lilies take longer. When you think the flowers might be dry, gently remove one as a test. If the petals seem crisp, remove the others. If not, let them dry a little longer. If the sand or borax clings to the petals, gently brush them with a camel's-hair brush. Fasten on the longer wires and store the flowers in a clean box until you want to use them.

Pressing

You will want foliage for your dried arrangements, and there are three ways to preserve it. The first is by Pressing. You use this method for ferns, autumn leaves, dogwood foliage, and other tree foliage. Put the material to be dried on several layers of absorbent paper—paper toweling or newspapers—making sure that the leaves are flat and not overlapping. Then cover it with more layers of paper and put a heavy weight on top. Books like the Encyclopaedia Britannica are good to use. The leaves' will take about three weeks to dry.

The second method of preserving foliage is to stand it in a *Drying* solution made of one-third glycerin and two-thirds water. The *Solution* liquid should be three to five inches deep. Crush or slit the ends of the branches, so that there is more area to absorb the mixture. When tiny beads of moisture appear on the leaves, the foliage is ready to use. This will take from a few days to two weeks. The leaves will change color, and will be supple. You can use them over and over again. When they are not in use, store them in a plastic bag in a cool place.

With flat leaves like ivy or galax, immerse them in the solution and soak them flat.

It is always fun to experiment with preserving living material, and if there is some foliage that you think would be pretty but isn't on any of the lists for glycerined material, why not try it? You may come up with something really unusual.

Large single leaves like magnolia, canna, rubber plant, and *Hanging* aspidistra can be dried either hung upside down in a warm dry place, or laid flat on a surface where air can circulate underneath. A cake or broiler rack can be used for this. The edges of the leaves may curl, or they may twist, but this just makes their form more beautiful.

To use these single dried leaves, fasten pieces of wire through the bottom long enough to double back and twist together. This makes a pliable sturdy stem, and makes it easy for you to place them for the best effect in your design.

Branches like podocarpus or broom will dry in curves if you cut them while they are dormant, and tie them to heavy wire bent in the shape you want. You can see how this has been done with broom in Fig. 8.

Use dried materials for arrangements just as you would fresh. In some ways it is easier to use, because you can bend the wire "stems" in any direction, and can stick them directly into a firm substance like Styrofoam, Oasis, or florist's clay. Make sure that it is well anchored. If you use a pinholder, and the wire stems are thin, you can put little pieces of clay between the needles for more support.

You can have very colorful arrangements with the dried flowers which retain their natural color by using them with treated or dried foliage. The glycerined leaves will be in shades from warm brown to golden tan, while the dried leaves are mostly in duller shades of brown or gray. You might have an arrangement in shades of rose and blue by combining cockscombs, pepper berries, strawflowers, hydrangeas, delphiniums, blue sage, and statice, or one in shades of yellow, orange, and brown, with strawflowers, beech leaves, cockscombs, yarrows, Chinese lanterns, goldenrod, and magnolia leaves. The combinations are only limited by your imagination.

These colorful dried arrangements are particularly appropriate for houses with period furniture and decoration—Georgian, French, and Victorian. They were widely used in the early days of this country, and have been made famous with the restoration of Williamsburg.

Arrangements of pods, cones, and dried branches, bold in form and brown, gray, or green in color are suitable for modern or contemporary decoration. Pods have a wonderful variety of interesting shapes. Yucca pods are like dark brown bells, milkweed is boat-shaped, and locust pods are long, narrow, and curved. When these are combined with linear material—manzanita branches, driftwood, large dried leaves like canna, magnolia, or rubber plant—the effect is like a piece of bronze sculpture.

Wall panels or plaques, using pods and cones, make stunning decorations for rooms of contemporary design. To make one, first decide on the size and shape you want, and choose a background to make it on. This can be a panel of wood or wall board, or a mat of burlap, monk's cloth, heavy linen, bamboo, or straw. Next plan the design as you would for a flower arrangement, with a definite pattern and center of interest. Assemble the different parts on a separate piece of paper, until it is the way you want it. Then sketch the design on the background, and fill it in piece by piece from the paper. If your background is of wood, fasten the material with glue. If you are using cloth, straw, or bamboo, you can wire or sew on the pieces.

It is fascinating to make pictures for a wall, or miniatures for a table, with dried material. For the pictures, be on the lookout at antique shops for small frames of the shadowbox type, or old-fashioned oval ones. If they are a little the worse for wear, never mind. They will be less expensive, and some paint and glue will restore them. Cover a piece of thin wood or heavy cardboard, cut to fit the frame, with velvet, grosgrain, silk, or cotton in a color you want for the background of your picture. Then, paying particular attention to scale, assemble a bouquet or nosegay of dried or pressed flowers on the background. This is usually done in spray effect, with the stems making part of the picture. When you have the flowers placed the way you want them, pick up each one, and paint the back of it with glue, using a water-color brush. If the flowers are very small, it will help to handle them with tweezers. When the glue is dry, fit the background in the frame.

For a miniature, use a small frame like the oval gold-colored ones you can find in a five-and-ten, or an antique miniature or daguerreotype frame. Then follow the same procedure as for the pictures, except use tiny flowers and grasses, again being particular that each is in proper scale to the other and to the size of the frame.

When I was redecorating my youngest daughter's bedroom I needed a rather large lamp for a round piecrust table, and I didn't want to buy one if I could help it. I thought of making one out of a glass apothecary jar. Inside the jar I put a miniature Victorian vase filled with a bouquet of tiny old-fashioned flowers—dried lilies of the valley, forget-me-nots, violets, miniature roses, statice, and field grasses. I made as much of the arrangement as would slide through the opening at the top of the jar outside. Then I put some Stickum on the bottom of the vase and gently lowered it into the jar, pressing it down firmly so that the Stickum would adhere to the bottom of the jar. Then with tweezers I finished the arrangement. My husband bored a hole in the stopper of the jar to hold the electric fixture, and I bought a plain white shade. By featuring the dried bouquet, I had a charming and rather unusual lamp that was unbelievably inexpensive.

A friend recently inherited a lovely old silver watch that opens in three panels. She covered the middle panel with velvet, and glued a spray of tiny dried flowers to it. This she uses as a most intriguing ornament on the bedside table in her guest room.

Perhaps dried material will be the answer to a decorating problem for you.

FLOWERS AND BERRIES SUITABLE FOR ARRANGEMENTS TO DRY BY HANGING

Pink, Red, and Rose	*Yellow and Orange*	*Blue, Lavender, and Purple*	*White and Gray*
Astilbe	Bittersweet	Astilbe	Artemisia
Bamboo	Chinese Lantern	Bachelor's Button	Astilbe
Blue Sage	Cockscomb	Globe Amarinth	Bayberry
California Pepper	Goldenrod	Heather	Desert Holly
Clover	Strawflower	Hydrangea	Honesty
Cockscomb		Joe-Pye Weed	Pearly Everlasting
Heather		Statice	Pussy Willow
Hydrangea		Thistle	Queen Anne's Lace
Red Salvia			Snow-on-the-Mountain
Rose hips			
Statice			
Strawflower			

FOLIAGE SUITABLE FOR GLYCERIN SOLUTION

Bayberry
Beech
Dogwood
Galax
Ivy
Laurel
Leucothoe
Magnolia
Maple (Japanese)
Rhododendron
Viburnum

PLANT MATERIAL SUITABLE FOR DRIED ARRANGEMENTS AND WALL PLAQUES

For Line	*Seed Pods*	*Other Material*
Broom	Baptisia	Acorns
Canna leaves	Cotton	Cattails

For Line	*Seed Pods*	*Other Material*
Castor Bean leaves	Iris	Coconut calyxes
Date Palm sprays	Jacaranda	Dock
Dried fern	Lily	Dried Mullein heads
Driftwood	Locust	Dried Okra
Galax leaves	Lotus	Embryo Palms
Magnolia leaves	Paulownia	Fungi
Manzanita branches	Rose Mallow	Gourds
Palmetto	Thistle	Lichens
Palm spathe	Trumpet Vine	Nuts
Rubber Plant leaves	Tulip Tree	Pine cones (many varieties)
Sea Grape leaves		Sweet Gum balls
Sea Oats		Wood roses
Wisteria vine		

ARRANGEMENTS OF WILDFLOWERS

FOR MOST of us the word wildflower is nostalgic. We remember the thrill, when we were children, of finding the first
spring violets, of seeing a pink carpet of spring beauties in the
woods, or masses of bluebells by a winding river. Although wildflowers have botanical names, the ones by which we know them
best are the affectionate descriptive ones they were given long ago
by people who loved them. Just to say "jack-in-the-pulpit," "butter
and eggs," or "buttercup" brings a picture of the flower to your
mind.

Nature has been lavish with these flowers. No cultivated garden
can compete in abundance with fields white with daisies, yellow
with mustard and buttercups, red with clover, or pink and purple
with joe-pye weed and wild asters. Because of their abundance we
are apt to think of them as commonplace and ignore the very real
beauty they have.

Dainty Queen Anne's lace, looking like a magnified snowflake,
is so taken for granted that it often goes unnoticed, although its
cultivated cousin, blue lace flower, is a big seller in florists' shops.
You can see how effective it is in the arrangement in Fig. 13.
White field daisies make as cheerful a bouquet in summer as hothouse marguerites do in winter. Wild catbrier grows in as intriguing curves as a carefully nurtured clematis vine. Goldenrod, whose
yellow plumes line roadsides in the fall and turn fields into waving
seas of gold, is hybridized in England and prized as a garden flower.
Goldenrod, incidentally, has been maligned for years because many
think its pollen is responsible for hay fever. It is interesting to know

Arrangement by Mary Alice Roche

Figure 13. Delicate Queen Anne's lace, one of our best-loved wildflowers, is used here in an antique container to make a beautiful arrangement. (Photo by Roche)

that a recent theory claims the pollen of goldenrod is too heavy to 'blow widely on autumn winds, and that other flowers and grasses blooming at the same time are really the hay fever culprits. In more tropical locations, wild "floppers" as shown in Fig. 14 are intriguing.

One of the things that is the most fun to do in spring, summer, and fall is to combine a picnic with a pilgrimage to gather wildflowers. Before you go on one, though, there are several important things to consider. First of all, all fields and woods belong to *someone* and before you open your picnic baskets and gather flowers, you should find the owner and ask his permission. Secondly, some of our most beautiful wildflowers are becoming rare almost to the point of extinction, and these must be conserved. Know the flowers which are on conservation lists, and don't pick them. The Wildflower Preservation Society in Washington, D.C., publishes a comprehensive list and you can write for this. Also become familiar with poisonous plants like poison ivy and poison oak, so that you can keep your distance from them and not remember your picnic in misery. And lastly, leave the woods in the same condition in which you found them.

Recently this was dramatically brought home to some people who live in a neighboring town. They had a gay picnic in some woods by a waterfall, unknowingly observed by the man who owned the property. Although they hadn't asked his permission, he didn't mind the fact that they picked bouquets of wildflowers, but he did mind that when they left the area was littered with papers, bottles, banana peels, and other debris. He took the number of their license plate, found out where they lived, and the following Sunday drove to their home on a fashionable suburban street. As the owners, entertaining guests on the terrace, watched aghast, the man proceeded to dump trash on the manicured lawn. When they remonstrated, he said, "I am just returning the things you forgot and left on my property last week."

Because you are apt to pick wildflowers at a distance from home, it is wise to take a container of water with you. Put a pail in the back of the car, or carry a jar of water in your flower basket. If you don't want to carry water, take some plastic bags with a little water in the bottom, put the flowers in them, and close the top so that there will be humidity inside. Pick the flowers as they are approaching their prime.

Arrangement by Katherine N. Cutler

Figure 14. An arrangement of pinky red "floppers" (bryophyllum) with
pittosporum and loquat leaves suitable for a porch. (Photo by Thomas W.
Hall, Bermuda)

Wildflowers seem to like an extra drink, so allow a little more time for them to harden than for other flowers. Some wildflowers are very sturdy and others are more fragile. By putting them in water immediately, and keeping them overnight before I arrange them, I have had good luck with many that are supposed to wilt quickly, like spring beauties, wild geraniums, and primroses.

Some people think that because a flower comes from the woods, fields, or roadside that it should automatically be arranged in an earthy container like a rough basket or a bean pot. Nothing could be further from the truth. The rule of "suitability of flowers and container as related by color, form, and texture" applies to wild-flowers as well as cultivated ones. Sturdy bright black-eyed Susans *would* be suited to a bean pot, but fragile, delicate bluebells would certainly be out of place in one. Violets, with their rich velvety texture and dainty form, look better in crystal than in a coarse tumbler. Some wildflowers seem suited to both simple and fine containers. Daisies, for instance, because of their pert look and bright yellow centers look well in a basket. But, because of the refined satiny texture of their petals, they are also suited to fine china.

It is fun to walk along a country road and get flowers for a mixed bouquet. In a short time you might find black-eyed Susan, wild snapdragon, butterfly weed, clover, Queen Anne's lace, and some interesting grasses. A flower arranging friend, visiting me from California, said, "I think I'll take a walk along the road and see what I can find in New Jersey for an arrangement for your party today." In twenty minutes she was back with a beautiful fall bouquet of wild aster, goldenrod, boneset, joe-pye weed, wild purple viburnum berries and red viburnum foliage, and purple blackberry·vine. Arranged in an antique brass wood bucket it was much admired by people who said, "And you *really* found all this along the roadside?" The arrangement in Fig. 22 is the result of a walk along Bermuda roadsides.

You would think that wildflowers at the seashore would be very rugged and sturdy to stand the high winds and salt spray—and I guess they are—but in appearance they are deceptively fragile-looking, and among the most beautiful. Among the first to appear is the beach plum—a drift of dainty white flowers over the dunes. Then follow beach peas, like miniature pink, white, and purple sweet peas, with gray-green vines and tendrils. There are delicate pink wild roses, fragile blue irises, and exquisite pink, red, and white mallows—cousins of the tropical hibiscus.

I glory in the mallows while they are in bloom, for I have found them so satisfactory for arrangements. Many people think that because the blossoms last only a day, and because there is so much foliage and stem in proportion to the flower, that it is hard to use them. But, like the hibiscus, they will last out of water for a day— so all the season that they are in bloom, I have a background arrangement of greens, and then I wire the mallow heads to florist's picks of different sizes and stick them in the green arrangement any place I wish. You can also use them in an effective way with driftwood, by just placing the flower heads so that they emphasize the line. It takes only a minute or two each morning to replace the wilted flowers with fresh ones.

There is one time that it is permissible to gather wildflowers that are on the rare list. This is when you know the property where they are growing is about to be cleared for developing or building. In fact, the most satisfactory thing to do, if you can, is to dig up the whole plant and bring it home and plant it, rather than have it fall victim to a bulldozer. If there is a corner of your yard that is shady or wooded, and the soil is acid, it will be similar to its natural habitat. The wild azalea, trillium, bloodroot, and columbine in my garden would have been destroyed long ago if I hadn't noticed builders' stakes in some neighboring woods and rescued the plants before the bulldozers arrived.

When wildflowers are growing on your own property, you can feel free to cut them for arrangements. In many flower shows conservation material is allowed if it is accompanied by a statement that it was grown by the exhibitor.

An attractive decoration for the house is a terrarium. This is a collection of little wild plants growing in soil in a glass container. Good containers to use are a fish bowl, a candy or apothecary jar, a bowl with a small opening at the top, a brandy snifter or a goblet. You can use a single plant in an attractive glass bottle. For plants you could use ferns, evergreen seedlings, miniature ivies, wild geraniums, partridge berries, wintergreens, bunch berries, small wild violets, and hepaticas.

To make the terrarium, line the bottom of the container with moss, green side out, and bring it part way up the container to hide the soil in which you will place the plants. Next, put some coarse gravel and pieces of charcoal in the bottom for drainage, and cover it with soil to the depth of an inch. A good mixture is one-third leaf mold, and two-thirds humusy garden dirt. So that the plants can be on different levels for a more interesting picture, make a mound or two of pebbles and pack soil around them.

Now assemble your plants, together with some objects that will add interest—a pretty rock, lichen-covered bark, little pieces of wood like miniature stumps, or a piece of fungus, and plan the design you want by placing them on a piece of newspaper. Put the taller plants toward the back, and be sure to have a center of interest. When they are arranged to suit you, put the little plants in the container in the same position you had them on the newspaper.

Pack soil firmly around the roots. Then cover the soil with moss. Spray the plants with an atomizer, making sure there is no dirt left on the leaves. Then cover the container. If it doesn't have a cover of its own, you can use a piece of glass. The moisture in the terrarium is governed by the cover. When the sides of the container are clouded and beaded with moisture, remove the top until the excess water has evaporated. As long as the glass is clear, leave the cover on. If the dirt gets very dry, spray it again. Keep the terrarium in a good light, but not direct sunlight. You will be fascinated to see the little plants growing before your eyes.

There is great satisfaction in gathering wildflowers, because most of us, whether we admit it or not, love "getting something for nothing" whether it is flowers for an arrangement, or wild straw-berries for jam. However, if you want wild plants for your garden or for a terrarium that are on the rare and conservation lists, there are excellent nurseries specializing in wild plants, where you can buy them.

Below is a list of some of the more familiar wildflowers. The ones in the first list are rare, and should not be picked. The ones on the second list may be picked moderately, and the ones on the third list can be picked freely.

Save

Bittersweet	Columbine	Ginseng
Bluebells	Dogwood	Ground Pine
Cardinal Flower	Gentian	Hepatica

Save

Holly
Lady's Slipper
Maidenhair Fern
Mountain Laurel
Orchids

Partridgeberry
Pipsissewa
Pitcher Plant
Prince's Pine
Rhododendron

Solomon's-Seal
Trailing Arbutus
Trillium
Walking Fern

Pick Discriminately

Anemone
Bellflower
Bloodroot
Blue-eyed Grass
Blue Flag
Bluets
Bush Honeysuckle
Butterfly Weed
Dogtooth Violet

Dutchman's-Breeches
Huckleberry
Marsh Marigold
Mayapple
Mistletoe
Shadbush
Sheep Laurel
Spring Beauty
Star-of-Bethlehem

Tulip Tree
Turtlehead
Violets
Water Lily
Wild Ageratum
Wild Geranium
Wild Rose
Wintergreen

Pick Freely

Black-Eyed Susan
Boneset
Bouncing Bet
Bush Clover
Butter-and-Eggs
Buttercup
Clover
Daisy
Dandelion
Day Lily

Goldenrod
Jewelweed
Joe-Pye Weed
Mallow
Milkweed
Morning Glory
Mullein
Mustard
Pickerelweed
Pokeweed

Queen Anne's lace
Skunk Cabbage
Sunflower
Sweet Clover
Tansy
Thistle
Wild Aster
Yarrow

ARRANGEMENTS USING HOUSEPLANTS

THERE are times when it is practical to use a houseplant for decoration rather than cut flowers. At certain times of the year in many parts of the country, flowers are scarce and expensive. There may be one of those crescendos in family life when you have no time to plan and arrange successive flower arrangements. You may be a career woman with a seasonal rush of work that leaves you little time for the housekeeping part of your life. And yet you want your rooms to have the indefinable air of graciousness that living plant material gives. This is the time to gratefully turn to houseplants.

You don't have to have an elaborate floor or window garden, lovely though these are. By choosing a container that is imaginative, and placing it where it can be dramatized by other accessories, you can make a single ordinary plant a most decorative feature. In the picture in Fig. 15 one of the most available and easiest to grow houseplants—philodendron cordatum—is planted in a brass teakettle and placed on a teakwood stand. The choice of container and stand transforms a rather commonplace plant into a distinctive decorative feature. The nice part is that it will continue to be lovely with very little care, just some water, a little food, and an occasional syringing of the leaves to keep them free of dust and insects.

In Fig. 29 it is the choice of the beautiful antique compotes as containers that makes an arrangement of ferns such a lovely decoration in an eighteenth-century bedroom.

Potted plants are a godsend to use on a dining table in winter, when admittedly it is a problem to find flowers for a centerpiece.

Figure 15. This is a good example of the imaginative use of a container not originally designed for plants. Here philodendron planted in a brass kettle placed on a small stand makes an unusual window-sill decoration. (Photo by Roche)

Here again it is important to choose distinctive containers, and you do have to choose plants that will grow without direct sunlight. Holly fern is one of these. I always associate holly fern with a mad dog, and this is why. When I was a small child my four-year-old sister was bitten by a mad dog. For twenty-three days she had to be taken every day from our small town to New York, fifty miles away, for Pasteur treatment. In those days this aroused a great deal of interest and sympathy, and she was showered with presents, and even the rest of the family got some. A friend gave my mother four charming squat silver monogrammed flowerpots. From that time on, every year of my childhood, from fall to spring, these pots, filled with holly fern, formed the centerpiece of our dining table.

One woman I know, whose house is very formal, uses a very beautiful centerpiece when she gives a dinner party in the winter. She happens to grow many varieties of African violets under artificial light in her basement. At the time of a party she fills a particularly handsome deep Sheffield compote with pots of violets —deep purples in the middle, and others ranging from the blue and lavender shades to rose and pink on the outside. Placed between silver candelabra, this is a fascinating centerpiece.

There are wall brackets sold commercially that, filled with plants, are stunning on the plain walls of a contemporary or Spanish-type house. They are usually made of wrought iron in the shape of vines and leaves, and have round metal circles attached to hold pots. I know of a house where the only decoration in a rather small dining room is one of these fixtures sprawling over one wall. The pots, holding trailing philodendron, are of yellow glazed pottery, matching the color of the seats of the chairs. The effect is unusual, refreshing and gay.

A hanging basket of growing plants arranged for artistic effect makes a conversation piece for a patio, porch, or terrace. You should make sure, in planning such a basket, that the plants you select will survive under the same growing conditions. To make one, buy a basket, such as a wire or openwork-straw one from a florist, and line it with moss placed with the green side out, or with layers of sphagnum moss. Then fill it to within an inch or two of the top with good garden soil mixed with some peat moss. Put the unpotted plants directly in the soil, arranging them for color and effect, and press the soil firmly around the roots. Check the soil daily to see if it is dry. If it is, water thoroughly, so that it gets to the roots. Plants that are exposed to the wind need watering more frequently than sheltered ones. Pinch back the plants to give them a better shape. You might use plants like ivy geranium, begonia, tuberous begonia, fuchsia, and foliage plants like tradescantia, various ivies, vinca, maranta, and ferns.

It would be amusing to have on a cool sheltered corner of your porch a large shallow oval pan painted with satin-black paint to give it a smooth patina and plant it with different varieties of ferns. Perched on some rocks in the middle of this miniature bower you might have a little figure of Pan, painted with the same black paint.

Sometimes in a house there will be a window sill that is ideal for growing plants, in a room that doesn't need decoration. It might be a utility room, a pantry, or a heated sunny garage. This is a wonderful place to have a miniature cutting garden—a place where you can grow houseplants which you can cut for arrangements like the coleus in Fig. 16. A little sprig of blooming begonia may be just what you need for the focal point in a miniature arrangement like the one in Plate 2. Or on the night you're having a very dressy dinner party, you can cut some leaves of rose geranium to float in the finger bowls. Some leaves of syngonium or angel wing begonia may be just what you need for an important focal point.

Houseplants need much the same care that we do. They must have food, water, and fresh air. They need to be bathed and groomed. They like rest periods, and they seem to respond to affectionate care. Believe it or not, more plants die from over-

Arrangement by Myra Brooks

Figure 16. Sprigs of coleus cut from a houseplant are used here in the focal point in an arrangement of leucothoe branches in an Oriental container with an Oriental accessory used for emphasis. (Photo by Roche)

watering than underwatering. A good way to tell whether a plant needs watering is to feel the soil at the top of the pot. If it feels dry to your fingers, it probably needs water. Fill the space from the top of the soil to the rim of the pot with water, let it seep in, and repeat until no more water is absorbed and air bubbles have stopped rising.

Spray the foliage of most plants (African violets are an exception) with water. It creates more humidity, improves their appearance, and helps them breath by keeping them free of dust. It also helps to keep them free of pests.

Feed plants by following the directions on the plant food you can buy at a florist's, and establish a regular feeding pattern. Just as you wouldn't give your children a large dose of vitamins one week, and skip giving them for several, it isn't good to give plants a big feeding so that they take a big spurt and then limp along for a while. Feed plants when the soil is moist, as obviously the food will then be distributed more quickly.

Arrangement by Mary Alice Roche

Figure 17. Bright coral geraniums make a charming color contrast to a charcoal ceramic container. (Photo by Roche)

You can take many foliage houseplants out of the pots and use them for arrangements as though they were cut flowers. The roots continue to grow in water, or, if you are using single leaves, many will root themselves. You select the combination you want according to color, texture, and form. You might use Chinese evergreen, sansevieria, or dracaena for height, with trailing vines of pothos, ivy, tradescantia. Some of the oddly shaped philodendron, rex begonia, or syngonium would make a distinctive center of interest.

Sometimes when a houseplant such as a geranium has grown thin and leggy, it is best to cut it drastically. Then you can choose a distinctive container and make an arrangement using the cut material. This was done in the arrangement in Fig. 17.

Here is a list of plants suitable for decoration and the locations they grow best.

South Window—Sunlight

Abutilon	Gardenia	Otaheite Orange
Anthurium	Geranium	Poinsettia
Azalea	Hibiscus	Primrose
Cactus	Jade Plant	Shrimp Plant
Crown of Thorns	Jerusalem Cherry	Thunbergia
Cyclamen	Morning Glory	

East or West Window—Good Light

Abutilon	Dracaena	Peperomia
African Violet	Echeveria	Piggyback Plant
Begonia	Fuchsia	Podocarpus
Caladium	Gloxinia	Spider Plant
Christmas Cactus	Maidenhair Fern	Succulents
Chrysanthemum	Maranta	Thunbergia
Coleus	Mimosa Pudica	

Least Light

Aspidistra	Fittonia	Philodendron
Baby's Tears	Grape Ivy	Pothos
Boston Fern	Holly Fern	Ribbon Fern
Chinese Evergreen	Kangaroo Vine	Sansevieria
Cyperus	Monstera Deliciosa	Schefflera
Dieffenbachia	Nephthytis	Spathiphyllum
English Ivy	Norfolk Island Pine	Syngonium
Fatshedera	Pandanus	Tradescantia

Plants Suitable to Be Featured as a Single Plant

Aspidistra	Crown of Thorns	Maidenhair Fern
Azalea	Cyclamen	Piggyback Plant
Begonia (several kinds)	Echeveria	Poinsettia
Boston Fern	Fuchsia	Primrose
Caladium	Gardenia	Shrimp Plant
Christmas Cactus	Geranium	Spathiphyllum
Chrysanthemum	Gloxinia	
Cineraria	Jerusalem Cherry	

MINIATURE ARRANGEMENTS

WHEN WE speak of a miniature arrangement, we generally mean one that measures less than five inches in any direction. It may be almost microscopic. The great challenge in making one is to have it in perfect scale. Sometimes a person will be intrigued with a miniature flower, and use it in a miniature arrangement without considering that although it is tiny in itself, it is too large in scale for the miniature container. You should be able to photograph a miniature arrangement and have the finished picture such that anyone looking at it would think it a full-sized arrangement. The photograph in Plate 2 is an illustration of this. The container is less than three inches wide, and the slender quince twigs and the begonia flowers and leaves at the focal point are in scale with it and with each other. The arrangement in Fig. 18 is also under five inches.

For anyone who likes tiny things, miniature arrangements are intriguing. It is fun to find and collect little objects that you can use for containers and bases. You can use your imagination and find plant forms that, translated to miniature, become others. For instance, a single floret of kalanchoe could be used as a miniature dahlia, black privet berries as black hothouse grapes, and a tiny side branch of blue sage as a tall stalk of delphinium.

Miniature arrangements should be seen at close range where their intricacies can be studied. They make wonderful gifts for invalids' bedside tables and trays. They can be unusual favors for a party table. For people who collect miniature furniture, a bouquet in proper scale to fit on a tiny table or desk is a highly

Arrangement by Catherine H. Smith

Figure 18. Some early spring fritillaria are used here to make a small arrangement suitable for a coffee table. (Photo by Roche)

prized acquisition. One woman I know completely decorated a friend's miniature living room for Christmas, as her present. She made miniature garlands for the mantel and doorway, a miniature Della Robbia wreath for over the fireplace, and a mass arrangement of greens and minute red berries in a tiny brass container for the top of a little chest of drawers.

Dried material in miniature arrangements has many uses. You can make place cards, Christmas cards, and Valentines featuring tiny dried bouquets glued in place. Miniature dried arrangements in lovely antique miniature or daguerreotype frames are exquisite decorative accessories.

It is fun, too, to make miniature fruit and vegetable arrangements. You could use a footed open salt for a container that would be a compote in miniature, and use rose hips for apples, Brussels sprouts for cabbages, privet berries for bunches of luscious-looking grapes, green acorns minus the shell for avocados, euonymous berries for tomatoes, pyrocantha berries for persimmons, and bittersweet berries for oranges. Wouldn't such an arrangement be just the thing to take to someone in the hospital at Thanksgiving time?

You have to think about the mechanics for miniature arrangements. A little piece of soaked Oasis filling the container is good because it not only holds the tiny stems, but it holds water for a comparatively long time. Because of their size, water evaporates quickly in tiny containers.

You can buy very tiny pinholders, and you can make these into cup pinholders by fastening them inside a screw bottle top. For miniature dried material, you can fill a bottle top with clay.

A list of suggested plant material, containers and bases for miniature arrangements follows.

Plant Material	Containers	Bases
Acacia	Doll china	Buttons
Acacia foliage	Egg cup	Driftwood
Alyssum	Liqueur glass	Frosted sea glass
Begonia	Open salt dish	Mirror
Bittersweet	Perfume bottle	Slate
Blue Sage	Scallop shell	Wood
Boxwood	Thimble	
Candytuft	Tiny basket	
Cedar berries	Tiny conch shell	
Coralbell	Toothpick holder	
Feverfew	Wine glass	
Fire Thorn berries		
Forget-me-not		
Gypsophila		
Heather		
Ilex		
Kalanchoe		
Lily of the Valley		
Miniature Ivy		
Miniature Rose		
Parsley		
Pepper berries		
Privet berries		
Salvia		
Vitex		

BUDGET ARRANGEMENTS

THE OTHER day a young bride said to me, "I would love to have fresh flowers in my home, but I live in a city apartment and have to buy them, and they seem like such a luxury item. Besides, when I go into a florist's shop I hesitate to buy less than a dozen flowers, or a single bunch, and yet I like a mixture. Does anyone ever go into a shop and say, 'I'd like two of these and three of those, and six of the ones over there'?"

My answer to her was, "They certainly do. And no one should ever hesitate to go into a shop and plan a mixed bouquet on the spot. Furthermore I have never run into a florist, thank goodness, whose interest or disinterest in a purchase was governed solely by its size."

Moreover, my young friend was wrong in thinking that fresh flowers are a luxury. Perhaps so, if she is thinking in terms of long-stemmed roses, and certainly so if she is lured by the low price into buying flowers from a street vendor, or in a shop other than a florist's. These may look fresh, but more often than not they will wilt overnight.

If you go to a reliable florist and learn which flowers give great value for the money you spend on them, and use imagination in your combination of flowers and container, it is possible to have fresh flowers without making a hole in your weekly housekeeping budget. Look for varieties that grow in sprays. Each stalk has several branches, and on them are flowers in all stages of development from buds to full blooms. This is true of spray chrysanthemums, freesias, yellow daisies, marguerites, and miniature carnations. They are fun to work with because you can snip off the fully opened flowers to use at the focal point, use the budded stems for line, and the partially opened flowers as a transition between the two. These flowers often last a week or two.

Heather is another economical flower. Because of the way it grows, with sprays tapering from a full cluster at the bottom to a thin end, you can have a mass arrangement without adding any other flowers. It lasts a long time, and when it dries is still lovely to add to a dried bouquet. A few sprays of yellow acacia will form a beautiful line arrangement, and can also be used after it dries.

When I was a bride, afternoon teas were very popular, and I remember one that I gave in honor of the visiting mother of a friend. My budget was low, it was winter, and the price of flowers was high. Moreover, you usually think of a large arrangement for a tea table. Feeling rather discouraged, I went into the florist's shop to

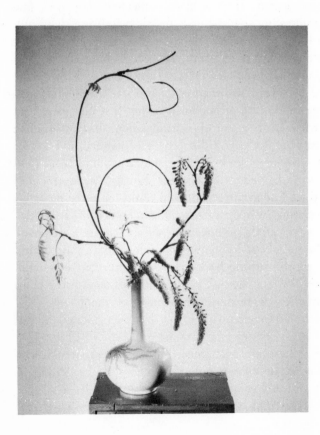

Arrangement by Myra J. Brooks

Figure 19. The fact that it is not necessary to use much plant material for a large arrangement is clearly demonstrated here. By imaginative choice of container and material, this arranger has achieved a dramatic effect with three wisteria branches and a few buds. Note how the eye is led in a complete circle around the arrangement, and how the strong reverse curves give distinctive impact. (Photo by Roche)

see what was available and noticed some lovely white freesias. They reminded me of some I had seen growing near a little garden pool in California, and suddenly I had an idea. One of my wedding presents had been an oval shallow container—creamy white pottery with a delicate blue lining. I bought a few sprays of freesia and arranged them with their foliage in two realistic clusters at the edge of my "pool" container, covering the pinholders with a few natural pebbles. Although it cost only a dollar, it pleased me so much that I've remembered it all these years.

In a living room, one perfect rosebud in a bud vase on a coffee table can give as much pleasure as a large bowl of roses. Never be hesitant about going into a shop and asking for just one rose.

When it comes to arrangements for a large space in a living room, such as a piano top or a place framed by a large wall area, think of flowers in terms of three instead of a dozen. You can get the bold sweeping lines you need with foliage or bare branches, and use three flowers for accent. If you have "collected" branches and dried vines of interesting shape, this is the time to bring them out. The picture in Fig. 19 shows how three dried wisteria vines can be the basis for a dramatic arrangement. If wisteria blossoms are not available, bougainvillaea, pepper berry, cockscomb, or heather are some that could be substituted for the same effect. In summer you can have a large interesting arrangement using just one variety of flowers. The trick is to make the arrangement distinctive like the one of garden iris done in the Japanese manner in Fig. 20.

You might buy foliage like broom or podocarpus and bend it in graceful curves as explained in the chapter "Foliage Arrangements." With this as a basic line arrangement, you could use three flowers— large chrysanthemums, tulips, or carnations as an accent. It is more interesting if you select these flowers in different stages of bloom. You can vary the form of a tulip and make it look like a large round open flower by gently turning back the petals with your fingertips. If you do it carefully, this doesn't injure the blossom, and it is an interesting form because it shows the center of the flower. The lowest tulip in the arrangement in Fig. 9 has been treated in this way.

The foliage in these arrangements will last several weeks, and you won't tire of it, because it will seem completely different as you vary the form and color of the flower accent.

The huckleberry which a florist often includes free of charge

Arrangement by Catherine H. Smith

Figure 20. A few stalks of iris cut from a perennial border can be used in an arrangement for a large space. The placement of the leaves and buds gives movement and rhythm to the design. (Photo by Roche)

with a flower purchase grows in a flat manner, and for this reason is well adapted to mantel arrangements. You might make twin arrangements in flat Chilean wine bottles or black Victorian urns. These are attractive using just the foliage, or you can give them an effective accent by adding a few flowers like three clusters of paperwhite narcissus or three sprays of begonia snipped from a houseplant.

For an interesting party table arrangement requiring few flowers, look over your collection of accessories. One or more of them can be the main feature of your centerpiece. This is true of the one using the palm spathe and coral fan in Plate 9. Instead of orchids, you could substitute a few sprays of heather, freesia, or miniature carnation.

Bird accessories make a good starting point. They might be ceramic ducks, china songbirds, or brass quail. Choose a suitable container and again use the tall branch idea. You could have driftwood, cattails, and grasses with the ducks, flowering branches for the china birds, and pine branches or autumn leaves for the brass quail.

If you have an interesting candelabrum, you can make it your centerpiece. Take out the center candle, and instead fasten a piece of soaked Oasis to the holder. (Details for doing this are described in Part III under "Buffet Tables.") It will take very few flowers combined with a little foliage to make a nosegay in the Oasis to bring freshness and fragrance to your table.

Fruit can be a double-purpose table arrangement. One January day I stopped by to see a young neighbor and found her preparing for a company dinner. "What can I do for a centerpiece?" she said. "I forgot about flowers, and I have only enough money left this week for food." I looked around her dining room and saw a pewter scale on the sideboard. "Don't I remember that you have a pewter compote?" I asked. She nodded affirmatively. I said, "Why not get some red apples and some grapes, and pick some of that green euonymus outside your door? Make arrangements of apples and grapes on the scale for the sideboard, and in the compote for the table, and after your company has gone you can use them for applesauce and Waldorf salad the rest of the week. That way you can make your food money double for your flower money."

These are only a few suggestions for the many ways to have fresh flowers in your house for little money. Perhaps they will lead you to ideas of your own that will not seem too luxurious for your budget.

(Photo by Roche)

Arrangement by Myra J. Brooks

PLATE I

An antique cheese tray is the container for this arrangement of marigolds, zinnias, nasturtiums, dahlias, and sage, and autumn colors. It would make a bright welcoming note in a hall, or would look equally well on a sideboard or buffet table.

Arrangement by Katherine N. Cutler

PLATE 2

Scale is important in this arrangement in a miniature three-inch container. The container is placed on a miniature scroll base. Twigs of forced Japanese quince are arranged in "heaven," "man," and "earth" positions, with blossoms and leaves of begonia at the base. This arrangement would be the proper size for a coffee table, or would bring a breath of spring to the bedside table of an invalid.

(Photos by Roche)

PLATE 3

Although the flower arrangement is but one of the components of a buffet table, it serves to tie the different parts together. Here, the flowers—lavender heather, purple anemones, yellow and white freesia, yellow acacia, blue irises, and coral azaleas—repeat the colors in the china and cloth.

The pewter container is related to the candelabrum, the salad bowl, and coffee service. It is also related in design to the china salt and pepper shakers, which in turn relate in design to the candelabrum. The candelabrum is placed off center to balance the visual weight of the flowers.

Lenox china courtesy Jane Smith Shops
Arrangement by Katherine N. Cutler

(Photo by Roche)

Arrangement by Marion Rowley

PLATE 4

Beech and mahonia foliage, which has been treated with glycerin, and celosia and globe amaranth, which were dried by the hanging method, form the material for this arrangement in an antique container. It is elegant and graceful, and will keep its glowing color indefinitely.

PLATE 5

It is fun to use Christmas tree balls and ornaments in arrangements at Christmas, but like any artificial material, they are most effective when combined with live plant material. Here arborvitae forms a spiral background for cascading Christmas tree balls that have been wired into clusters. Larger balls and small ornaments fill the tiers of the alabaster epergne.

(Photos by Roche)

PLATE 6

A damask cloth forms the background for gold and white china in this formal dinner table place setting. Pineapple, pears, apples, tangerines, and grapes, sprayed gold, are arranged with green limes and ivy geranium foliage in an S-curve design on an antique gold and white compote. This could be a place setting for a formal dinner party, a Christmas dinner table, or for a golden wedding anniversary.

Lowell plate courtesy Lenox China Arrangement by Katherine N. Cutler

Arrangement by Myra J. Brooks

PLATE 7

The name of the rose used here, Peace, might well be the title for this line mass arrangement. Note that the flowers are used in all stages of development, from tight bud to full-blown flower. Stems can be angled if a soaked piece of Oasis is wedged in the neck of the container, protruding an inch or so above the rim.

(Photos by Roche)

PLATE 8

The repeated curves in the globular base of the container seem to call for a circular design in this mass arrangement of garden flowers. Good balance is achieved with most of the white flowers at the outside edges, although white is carried from the nicotiana at the bottom, through the zinnias in the center, to the nicotiana and feverfew at the top for a good blending of color.

Arrangement by Myra J. Brooks

(Photo by Roche)

Arrangement by Mrs. J. Westford Cutler

PLATE 9

There is a tropical feeling in this setting designed for a terrace luncheon table. Several of the appointments were "collected"—the coconut spathe from Florida, sea fan from Bermuda, driftwood base from a New Jersey beach, natural oyster shell from a Baltimore fishing dock, crackle shell plate from California. Miniature cymbidium orchids, resembling pink coral, are combined with philodendron leaves in the arrangement.

Arrangement by Julia S. Berrall

PLATE 10

This arrangement for the center of a dining room table illustrates how flowers can be extended at the sides to give horizontal proportion. This eliminates the necessity of building up the height to a point where it would obstruct the view of people sitting across the table. Here the proper height is achieved with a thin line of buds. Note that the pinholder in the glass container has been concealed with foliage. Individual flowers are cut from the stem and grouped at the focal point.

(Photos by Roche)

PLATE 11

The colors in the apples and grapes in this fruit arrangement are repeated with the nosegays of anemones in the fluted smoke bells. The white of the containers is picked up with the tiny clusters of andromeda. This would be a stunning arrangement for a sideboard or a holiday buffet table.

Arrangement by Mrs. Harold Brooks

(Photo by Roche)

Arrangement by Myra J. Brooks

PLATE 12

That arrangements of dried material can be colorful is beautifully illustrated in this line mass bouquet of roses, strawflowers, delphiniums, celosia, and cobaea calyxes which have been dried and combined with glycerined foliage.

CORSAGES

A CHARMING way to show special attention to someone is to give a corsage or a nosegay. The arrival of a square glossy white florist's box containing a corsage is one of the greatest thrills of a girl's first big dance.

But it isn't only for big parties that a corsage seems the appropriate thing to give. You might want to pay a little special attention to a dear elderly friend by making her a corsage on Mother's Day. Or welcome a new baby by making a miniature nosegay to tuck in with flowers for his mother. (She could enjoy it on her bedside tray.) It is a gay bon voyage gift for an ocean traveler, who will enjoy it during vegetationless days at sea. It can be an added touch for an unusual occasion, such as the time a neighbor delighted a small girl who was "launching" her nine-foot sailboat by making her a corsage to wear for the ceremonies.

My memories of Easter as a child include along with jelly bean hunts and the smell of the black-dyed cotton of my choir robe, the little corsages of yellow daisies and bachelor's buttons that our mother always made for my sister and me to wear with our blue serge coats and leghorn hats to Sunday School.

On someone's birthday, a corsage to wear during the festivities makes a person of any age feel "special." It makes a nice way to welcome a guest of honor. Just recently I was with a group of young women who were making corsages for the new mothers at the first PTA meeting of the year—a gracious welcoming gesture, and at the same time a way of identifying those who were there for the first time.

A small corsage makes an unusual and pretty way to decorate special packages. They also make festive table favors—for example, you could use a single large chrysanthemum and some autumn leaves in a corsage for favors for a football luncheon.

Once you master a few little tricks of construction, corsages are not a bit hard to make. As for a flower arrangement, you start by choosing flowers and foliage that you want to use, and giving them a *long* drink of water. If they are well hardened, they will last for a reasonably long time out of water.

You will need scissors, 22- and 24-gauge wire, florist's tape and ribbon. Cut the stem of a flower with a large calyx as near to the calyx as possible. If you want to make doubly sure of the flower staying fresh, put a small piece of wet cotton over the cut stem end. Take a piece of wire about eight inches long, and run it through the bottom of the calyx near the stem, so that it extends equally on each side. Bring these ends down and twist them together to make a "stem." It will be strong and pliable. Then pinch the end of a piece of floral tape firmly around the top of the stem, and hold it there in your left hand. Wind the tape around the wire stem by twirling it with your right hand.

In the case of a flower without a prominent calyx, and a flat head, like a daisy, push the piece of wire up through the center of the flower, then bend it over and push it down through the center again. If the flower is a fragile type, and you don't want a double wire stem, cut the wire off after you have looped it through the center, so that what remains is a sort of hook on a single wire stem. Wind these stems with tape also.

A corsage is more interesting if you use some buds. Wire these with the finer wire, the same as the flowers. Wire leaves by hooking the wire through the base of the leaf.

When you have finished wiring all the flowers, buds, and leaves, assemble them in the design you want, making sure there is a center of interest, and wire them in position. Cover any exposed wire with tape.

A bow is attractive on a corsage but should be subordinate to the flowers. To make a bow, make two opposite loops of ribbon the size you want the finished bow, and follow with loops that get progressively smaller, making sure that the opposite loops are balanced in size. Pinch the middle together and tie it tightly with a separate piece of ribbon. Pull and twist the loops into a full bow, and tie it on the corsage with the ends of the piece you used to tie the center.

A nosegay is made differently from a corsage, in that each flower is wired individually, but the stems are not individually taped. A nosegay (called a Tussy Mussy in Victorian days—a horrible name for something delicate and lovely) is formed by making concentric circles of smaller flowers around a larger one in the middle. For instance, you might have a tea rose in the center, with circles of sweetheart roses and violets surrounding it. When you have arranged the little bouquet in your hand, twist a wire around all the stems, and tape the whole group as one. These nosegays are usually finished with a frill, which may be lace, lace paper, or ruffly leaves. Fragrant and spicy scented flowers are used, as it was the custom in Victorian days for young ladies to carry them to smell when they felt fashionably faint.

This type of nosegay is particularly appropriate for a flower girl at a wedding. One of the prettiest I have seen was made by a mother of the bride for her flower-girl granddaughter to carry. It was a circle of bouvardias around a gardenia, bordered with rose geranium leaves.

It is fun to experiment with different things at times when you are not actually making a corsage for a particular purpose. You may discover some fascinating and unusual combinations to use when you want to make one as a gift. Also, since plant material is alive, there is no infallible rule as to how long each variety of flower or leaf will last, and it is wise to experiment beforehand so that you can be sure your gift won't wilt shortly after it is received.

Flowers and foliage that are good to use in corsages and nosegays are:

Corsages		Nosegays	
Flowers	*Foliage*	*Flowers*	*Foliage*
Bachelor's Button	Bay Grape	Bouvardia	Begonia
Camellia	Galax	Daphne	Fern
Carnation	Grape Ivy	Garden Pink	Geranium
Chrysanthemum	Ivy	Garnet Rose	Ivy
Daisy	Laurel	Heliotrope	Mint
Day Lily	Oak	Lily of the Valley	Parsley

Corsages (cont.)		Nosegays (cont.)	
Flowers	*Foliage*	*Flowers*	*Foliage*
Gardenia	Pachysandra	Mignonette	
Gladiolus	Philodendron	Pansy	
Hibiscus	Pothos	Stephanotis	
Lace Flower	Rhododendron	Sweet Pea	
Lily	(individual leaves)	Violet	
Orchid			
Pansy			
Passionflower			
Rose			
Zinnia			

ARRANGEMENTS USING
ARTIFICIAL FLOWERS

THERE was a time, not too long ago, when an experienced flower arranger would have thrown up her hands in horror and said, "Heavens, no!" if she were asked if she ever used artificial flowers in an arrangement. In recent years, though, the art of making artificial flowers has been so perfected that many of them are exquisite and look so real that it is only when you touch them that you know they are not. Although there are still a few diehards holding out, most experts admit there is a place for artificial flowers in today's arrangements. I was secretly amused not long ago when a lecturer who was using some in her demonstration arrangements couldn't bring herself to say "artificial flowers" and kept referring to them as "permanent material."

No matter how well it is made, however, an artificial flower can't equal a real one. The principal reason is that the real flower is living and breathing, and the artificial one is not. There is no slight movement of petal or leaf. It is completely static. Sometimes when you first see a bouquet of artistically arranged artificial flowers in a room you may think, "I defy anyone to know that it isn't real." But when you stay in the room and look at it for a while, you become conscious of the difference.

I am thinking of one in particular. When I first saw it in the house of a friend, I thought, "How lovely!" Now, after seeing it in the same place for two years, looking exactly the same, I am completely bored with it. A big argument against using artificial arrangements is that people tend to regard them like pictures on a wall and, once they are placed, leave them indefinitely. This is fine for a picture—it is an art form in which there is always something new to see—but with a flower arrangement much of the charm comes from its living quality, and I think subconsciously we resent it when it is static.

For this reason, if you do want to use artificial flowers, why not have a collection of the ones you prefer and bring different ones out from time to time to use with real foliage? In this way you get the color and form of the flowers, but the arrangement isn't static. For instance, there are completely real-looking rhododendron blossoms on the market. Rhododendron foliage is available most of the year, but it is possible to have the real blossoms for only a short season. So, for an arrangement of flowering rhododendron, wire the artificial blooms to the real foliage. The same applies to dogwood. You can buy very real-looking individual dogwood blossoms and wire them onto a living branch. It is difficult to have geranium plants bloom in the house in winter, but the leaves grow luxuriantly. A row of these plants on a window sill, wired with bright artificial flowers, would be attractive.

You can also use this live and artificial combination with fruit. As anyone who likes to do fruit arrangements knows, you are limited by seasonable material. The very thing that you need most to accent the arrangement may not be in the market. If you keep an assortment of very real-looking artificial fruit on hand, you can add a bunch of purple grapes, a pomegranate, or a persimmon to your live arrangement, and no one will be the wiser. (I am not speaking of an arrangement for a flower show, of course.)

Most people have a definite color scheme for their dining rooms, carried through wallpaper, draperies, tablecloths, and china. Sometimes there aren't any flowers available for a table centerpiece in this color scheme. This is a time when it is convenient to have artificial flowers on hand of the proper size and color. Use them with real foliage, and you can have a most attractive centerpiece. But *please* don't leave it indefinitely.

There are some instances when artificial material all by itself can be a godsend. I have a friend who found this out when she bought a summer house with a two-storied living room. At one end is a massive stone fireplace with a chimney piece reaching to the ceiling. High above the mantel is a niche set in the stone. She was at her wit's end to know what to do with the niche, until she thought of artificial plants. She bought a long narrow container to fit the opening and filled it with artificial sansevieria, philodendron, bells of Ireland, and other greens. The effect is natural and stunning. It would be impossible to use real plants in this case. There isn't enough light for them to grow properly, and you would need to use a ladder every time you watered them.

Another place where artificial flowers could easily be the answer is a doctor's office or waiting room. These are busy places and there is usually no time to rearrange bouquets or care for houseplants. People may be nervous and apprehensive in such a room, and would much rather see a gay bouquet of artificial flowers than one that is depressingly droopy or a houseplant that is neglected. Besides, different people are constantly coming and going, and the arrangement isn't boring.

Artificial material is also fun for "tongue in cheek" decorating. I saw a clever use of it the other day in a guest apartment over a garage. The enclosed stairway leading to it, inside the garage, has open risers. So that mosquitos can't get into these openings from the garage space, the stairway is backed by screening. A decorator conceived the idea of putting artificial ivy between the screening and the stair risers. With the treads painted white, you now have the impression of climbing up white steps set into a bank of ivy.

Yes—there certainly are uses for artificial material—but *do* use fresh when you can.

III
Arrangements for a
House

PERIOD ARRANGEMENTS

A FLOWER arrangement should be suitable for the house in which it is placed. For the most part, houses in this country can be categorized according to some period of the country's development—Early American, Southern Colonial, Georgian, Dutch Colonial, Victorian, Spanish, and Contemporary. Under Contemporary there are really two classes—the houses sometimes called Modern, a development of this century using clean-cut lines and great expanses of glass, and the houses that are of no particular period but have features of several and are furnished with a comfortable accumulation of old and new belongings.

We know that from the time the first settlers came, people had gardens and decorated their houses with flowers. The styles in which they arranged them, the types of flowers, and the containers they used were governed by the location and manner in which they lived.

The early New Englanders were too busy struggling to grow food in the rocky soil to have a flower garden. The few flowers they did grow by their doorsteps were the result of cherished seeds and slips which they brought with them—bright sturdy flowers like geraniums and marigolds. How they must have rejoiced in the wealth of beautiful wildflowers and shrubs in the New England woods, and with what delight they must have filled their utilitarian containers—iron pots, pewter bowls, stone jugs, and wooden kegs—to bring color and cheer into their dark cabins with gay wildflowers.

It was quite different, on the other hand, for the settlers in the southern colonies. These were the wealthy traders, who had slaves to cultivate their flower gardens as well as their cotton and tobacco. Because of the temperate climate, plants grew easily, and in addition to the native ones, rarer plants and bulbs were imported from abroad. Also imported were containers of fine china, silver, and Chinese porcelain. These were usually in the shape of a wide-mouthed bowl or a classic urn, and were well suited to the elegant mass bouquets of roses, lilies, carnations, tulips, and stock that decorated rooms filled with beautiful furniture and fabrics.

At this time too they imported furniture, fabrics, and china from France. Flower containers from France were slender and graceful vases of porcelain, or delicately carved urns of alabaster. Bouquets with a French influence, though still of the mass type, were more airy and feathery. The flowers were of pastel shades to go with the dainty furniture and pale silk fabrics.

In the Victorian period, furniture became heavy and dark. Fabrics were thick and richly colored, and rooms were filled to bursting with ornaments, bric-a-brac, pictures, and statues. Many new flowers had been introduced because of expanding world trade, and the mass arrangements of that period reflected the "business" of the general décor. Containers were decorated with paintings or raised gold designs. They were also made of many types of glass—Bristol glass, Sandwich glass, milk glass, and satin glass. The typical Victorian container was a flat fan-shaped china vase, decorated with gold and flowers. It is this type that we usually mean when we speak of a Victorian vase today. A vase like this was crowded with a round mass of many kinds of flowers—pansies, roses, violets, pinks, heliotrope, with pendulant flowers like bleeding hearts or fuchsia hanging down from the sides of the vase. Almost always some wildflowers and grasses were included. However, it is also possible to have a Victorian-type arrangement using only one kind of flower, as shown in Fig. 21, where pink and red roses are combined with their buds and foliage to make the typical period design.

The Spanish settlers of the Southwest brought heavy carved furniture and colorful utensils—tall pottery jars, copper baking pans, copper milk jugs, and wrought-iron trays—to put in square houses with thick white walls. These made perfect containers in scale and color for their tropical flowers—hibiscuses, bougainvillaeas, camellias, calla lilies, and bird-of-paradise.

The modern house, typical of this century, has large areas of bare wall, often of wood, and ceiling-to-floor expanses of glass.

Arrangement by Myra Brooks

Figure 21. A Victorian arrangement of red and pink garden roses. Notice that the clever use of buds and foliage has given the characteristic outline of an arrangement of the period. (Photo by Roche)

The furniture is streamlined, and the colors are soft and muted. Arrangements in this type of house are simple but dramatic—bold in design and subtle in color, like the one in Fig. 22. For the other type of contemporary house, that of no particular period, there is a wide range of suitable arrangements. Any that are not deliberately designed according to a certain period and fit the color and scale of the general decorative scheme are fine.

The type of house should influence the type of arrangement used in it. While there is no rule that says you can't put an elegant eighteenth-century arrangement in a simple Early American house, it just wouldn't look as though it belonged. Nor would a fussy Victorian bouquet look well with the bare glass and wood interior

Arrangement by Katherine N. Cutler

Figure 22. Cut palmetto, false orange, purple palmetto berries, and yellow croton are arranged in a palm spathe to simulate a boat under sail. (Photo by Thomas W. Hall, Bermuda)

of a modern house. This doesn't mean that you are limited to arrangements absolutely authentic of the period. There are many variations in all periods of arrangement. But it does mean that you should consider the type of house you live in, its furnishings and décor, and be influenced accordingly when you choose flowers and containers.

ARRANGEMENTS FOR OUTSIDE
ENTRANCE AND HALL

ARRANGEMENTS of plants and flowers at the outside entrance of your home make a wonderful way to give a gracious welcome to visitors. There are many things that you could
use for containers, but they should be in keeping with the period
of the house.

One woman I know, whose house is Early American, uses an
iron grate (the kind that is made for burning coal in a fireplace)
on her doorstep. She changes the arrangement with the seasons. In
the spring there are flowering branches, in summer, wildflowers
and flowers from her garden, in the fall, branches of vivid autumn
leaves. At Hallowe'en there is a huge jack-o'-lantern surrounded by
smaller pumpkins. At Thanksgiving the grate is filled to overflowing with pumpkins, gourds, squashes, and Indian corn, and at
Christmas, with red poinsettias against a background of greens.
The poinsettias, since she lives in the North, are artificial. She
claims that it takes but a few minutes to arrange the material in
Mason jars which are concealed by the front of the grate. The
arrangement in Fig. 23 was made for the doorway of a Dutch
colonial house.

If your house is Victorian, you may be able to find at an auction
or a secondhand store a pair of the round metal urns that graced
many gardens around the turn of the century. These were usually
painted black, white, or dark gray-green. You can have metal containers made to fit them, and in them all summer have large
bouquets of garden flowers with trailing sprays of ivy spilling down
the sides. Or, you could plant them with begonias, ivy geraniums,

Arrangement by Myra Brooks

Figure 23. Dutch tulips are arranged in a pair of wooden Dutch shoes as a colorful door decoration. (Photo by Roche)

or fuchsia. In the winter they could hold a pair of small evergreen trees.

For an eighteenth-century house you might make a pair of tapered ivy trees. These look very impressive but are really quite simple to make. To do it, select matching pots—they may be of metal, pottery, or clay, either plain or painted. Make a cone of chicken wire the diameter and height that you want and fill it with moistened sphagnum moss. Sink the cones in the soil in the pots, and plant ivy around them. Also plant rooted ivy cuttings in the sphagnum moss in the cone. As the ivy in the pot grows, train it around the cone, and soon, with the cuttings, the wire will be covered, and you will have a pair of most decorative trees. When you water them, be sure to moisten the moss inside the cone also.

A ceramic lavabo, or terra-cotta wall pockets, would be attractive attached to the stucco walls of the Spanish-type houses of the Southwest. The soft green of succulents, spilling from these against the white or subtly colored walls, would make a fascinating combination of color or texture.

There are many other things you could use for containers at an outside entrance. There are garden jardinieres, old churns, brass coal scuttles, or large blown-glass bottles. And don't forget about baskets. These come in so many materials, shapes, and colors that your choice is practically unlimited.

Not many of us in these busy days have time to completely fill our houses with flowers every day. However, there is no room in which they don't belong, and you may want to make arrangements in different rooms on different days as your mood inspires you. Let's see what some of these could be.

The entrance hall is the first room that a visitor sees in your home. It is often the only room that a stranger ever sees, and it is the room that first welcomes the family home from daily trips to office, school, and market. The welcome should be a cheery one, and nothing can give this more than arrangements of flowers and plants. Even in the tiniest hall there is a place for living plant material.

One that I never enter without being impressed is a tiny elliptically shaped one, with stairs curving across the back. The only furnishing in the hall, and the thing that you see facing you as you open the door, is a wide shelf of handsome wood on brackets against the stair wall. On the shelf, in an interesting tall brass bottle with a narrow neck, is an arrangement of sansevieria leaves and pothos growing in water. The tall swordlike leaves of the sansevieria make an interesting contrast to the heart-shaped ones of the pothos trailing down the side of the bottle. The arrangement is flanked by two handsome large brass snails. The effect is dramatically simple, and very distinctive.

Arrangements of plants that grow in water are very practical in a hall, for they last a long time. You can arrange a variety of leaves and small plants with roots, as you would cut flowers. On the wall you might hang a pair of brass estribos like the one pictured in Fig. 12. A small jelly glass will fit inside to hold water. Put some charcoal in the water to keep it sweet. Variegated philodendron, whose leaves are marbled in ivory, would be attractive in these.

A narrow rectangular container of the shape usually known as a "planter" would be a good size and shape for a narrow hall table. In this you could have Chinese evergreen for height, graceful sprays of ivy at the sides, and coleus and begonia leaves for an interesting and colorful center of interest. All of these could be fastened to pinholders in the container. If you get ivy from outdoors, cut it before the weather is too cold, cut mature growth rather than the tempting new green tendrils, and douse the leaves under the faucet to free them of dust and insects.

In a hall that is large enough, there is nothing more cheerful than a bright splashy bouquet. Often a hall table is placed under a large mirror, and this is a challenging place for flowers. I say "challenging" because the flowers will be reflected in the mirror, and so the back of the arrangement must be as attractive as the front. You can accomplish this by making the arrangement as though it was to be seen only from the front. Then, when it is in place, take extra flowers and leaves and fill in the back, looking in the mirror as you do it to make sure that the reflected flower picture has good design. The arrangement in Fig. 24 is especially suitable for the entrance hall of a modern house, or one of Spanish type with high ceilings.

If, as in many halls, you are fortunate to have a small niche built into the wall, you have a little stage, and you can let your imagination have full rein setting little scenes. Maybe it's a terribly cold snowy winter, and you'd love to take off for the tropics, but you can't. Bring the tropics to you for a while by bringing out shells, starfish, sea fans, pieces of colored glass, and any other related things you have collected. Line the niche with a paper to suggest an underwater color, cover the floor of the niche with sand, find some green plant material that looks as though it might be underwater growth. (Small crinkly spinach leaves are one example.) Put this in a pinholder, and hide the holder with stones and shells. Experiment with placing your other objects until you have created a tropical underwater scene. Then when the sleet is pelting against the windows and you are feeling blue, go and stand in front of the niche, get a glimpse of the far South, and feel cheerful again.

Perhaps you have one of the many lovely figures of St. Francis with his birds. You can line the floor of the niche with moss, and make a shady glen for St. Francis to stand in, with pieces of foliage to simulate trees, and a few early hepatica or bloodroot blossoms nestled among the birds at his feet. (If you want to use just a few little flowers with a scattered appearance, you can buy tiny little pinholders, less than half an inch wide, and fasten them in screw tops of bottles, so that they can hold water. Hide them under the moss.)

Arrangement by Katherine N. Cutler

Figure 24. An arrangement of sansevieria, loquat leaves, screw pine, and the "locust and wild honey" fruit of the monstera, on a base of coral slabs. (Photo by Thomas W. Hall, Bermuda)

If you don't want to go to the trouble of making scenes in your niche, you could do what I do. In mine I usually keep two sentimental objects—a gray-blue Copenhagen narrow-necked vase that my youngest daughter brought me from her first trip abroad, and a little ceramic fledgling bird with upraised beak, in the same colors, that my ten-year-old grandson gave me last Christmas saying, "I hope you like it because it cost a whole dollar." This is where I put an especially pretty hybrid rose from the garden, a late spray from the climbers, or a few sprigs of unusual foliage that has caught my eye—in fact anything that I want to enjoy all by itself. The little bird, placed so that he is looking up at them, seems to enjoy them too.

ARRANGEMENTS FOR
THE LIVING ROOM

THERE is perhaps no place in a house, with the possible exception of the dining room table, that is more important to have flowers than the living room. A room may be decorated in perfect taste, but without some living plant material it can be as cold and impersonal as a store display. On the other hand, a cottage room furnished with nondescript hand-me-downs gives a lasting impression of coziness and charm if it features some distinctive flower arrangements.

Admittedly it takes time to arrange flowers, and most of us are busy with other activities. For this reason I think it is a very good idea to sit down and decide where in your living room flowers look best. Perhaps it is a table against a wall, an end table, or the top of a desk. Then deliberately choose containers that fit these places, are adaptable to several patterns of design, and are decorative even without flowers. If you then spend a little time studying the kinds of arrangement you want in them, and plan the mechanics, on a busy day you can whip up the arrangements in no time. And, if it is such a busy time that you haven't even a minute for flowers, the empty containers will be decorative in themselves.

I have two that I use all the time. One is the bronze lamp base that I have already described in the chapter on Containers, and stands on a mahogany pedestal table against a pale green wall. The other is a hexagonal fluted pewter sugar bowl, and is on a small oval end table. In the lamp base I can make arrangements of almost any design. In the sugar bowl, mass arrangements of garden flowers are best.

In the summer, which is my busiest time, I make an arrangement in the lamp base container of greens, such as euonymous, podocarpus, or laurel, which lasts a long time and acts as a background for flowers. I usually use hybrid day lilies, which I think are one of the most satisfactory flowers that ever bloomed. There is a succession of bloom from June to September, the form of the flower head is beautiful, and are in almost any shade you could possibly want to use—yellow, apricot, orange, mahogany, coral, crimson, scarlet, and many with combinations of these colors. The blossoms last only a day, but some time ago I made a big discovery. They last *out* of water as well as *in* water. Each morning I pick just the flower heads and wire them on florist's picks of assorted sizes. I stick them in the Oasis-filled container against the background of greens in whatever manner and color combination my mood of the day calls for. Sometimes it is a line mass, and sometimes a mass arrangement. Sometimes it is in shades of yellow, orange, and brown, and sometimes shades of pink to red, or sometimes a combination of many colors. It takes only a few minutes each morning to pull off the dead blooms and rewire fresh ones. If I am going to entertain at night, I put some blossoms in the refrigerator during the day, and they last through the evening.

In October the lamp base holds a mass arrangement of hydrangeas and branches of juniper loaded with pale gray-blue berries. This arrangement dries in place, and is interesting because the colors of the hydrangeas change as they dry, and each head contains many colors. It always reminds me of the afterglow of a pastel sunset, as pale pink, lavender, gray-blue, and pale green highlights appear in the bronze, reflected from the colors in the flowers above.

At Christmas time there is a line arrangement of gnarled pine branches, with sprays of red-berried holly as supporting lines, and a focal point of red poinsettias.

In the pewter sugar bowl, from June until the end of September, I have white hybrid petunias from my border. (It really isn't worth while planting petunias that aren't hybrid. There is very little difference comparatively in the cost of the plants, and a great difference in the size and perfection of bloom.) The texture of the petals of the petunia and the patina of the old pewter seem made for each other.

Of course there are times when you would want other arrangements in the room, but this method is a good way to insure always having fresh flowers although your time is limited.

Living room mantels are interesting places to put flowers. You can have twin vases at each end, or you can have an arrangement at one end, balanced by candlesticks or other appropriate accessories at the other. Sometimes it is fun to use twin containers near the center of a mantel, with a crescent design following the oval curves of a mirror or portrait that is hanging in the center.

There are many twin containers suitable for mantels. For Early American and Colonial houses, there are pewter mugs, cheese boxes, luster pitchers and bowls, and candle molds. For eighteenth-century houses there are Chinese porcelain bowls, porcelain urns in a classic shape, delicate bronze containers, and for Victorian, fan-shaped vases, metal urns with marble bases, alabaster compotes and figurines holding a small bowl aloft.

The arrangements in twin containers do not have to be identical. In fact it is much more interesting if they are not. They should be the same size, and the same in symmetry and balance, but there can be variation in color and placement of material. This is illustrated in the picture in Fig. 25. You will notice that in one, the focal point is emphasized by a cluster of sedum, and in the other by a cluster of pansies. These arrangements also illustrate how to have good balance in a container with a single handle, such as a mug or a pitcher. You will notice that the tallest point in the arrangement is on the handle side of the center, and the focal point is near where the handle joins the container. The line of design graduates from the tallest point down toward the spout and extends out from there. This gives the arrangement stability, by balancing the visual weight of the handle.

A living room coffee table is a popular place for flower arrangements. The important thing to remember when doing one is to keep the arrangement in proportion to the size of the tabletop. If it is a small table, you could make a miniature arrangement, but some coffee tables are quite large, in which case the arrangement would be larger too. It should never dominate the other accessories on the table but should be in proper scale with them. The material that you use, too, should have good scale relationship with the container.

In an Early American house you might use a pewter inkwell for a container, with an arrangement of miniature geraniums, or a pewter porringer with pansies. You might use a pressed-glass spoonholder with a bouquet of small garden flowers. In an eighteenth-century type living room, a small Oriental bowl with a mass arrangement of miniature roses would be appropriate. In a Victorian house, a vase shaped like a hand holding a cornucopia, typical of that period, would be just the thing for a little bunch of lilies of the valley, violets, or fuchsia. For the coffee table in a modern house why not use an opened ebony box, with three white cyclamen flowers and their heart-shaped leaves placed at one side, the blossoms poised like white butterflies against the upraised lid? Or you could arrange a few miniature iris with their pointed leaves in a cup pinholder on a flat wooden or metal plate.

Arrangement by Myra J. Brooks

Figure 25. These twin arrangements in pewter containers would be attractive at either end of a mantel, or at the ends of a dining table. Notice that twin arrangements, while similar in size and design, are more interesting if they are not identical in the placement of material. There is good relationship here of color and texture between plant material and container, for the flowers have the same velvety texture of the pewter, and the gray sedum reflects its color. (Photo by Roche)

A challenging thing to do in a living room is to complement a beautiful painting with a flower arrangement. In fact flower shows are now held in museums to do this very thing. The flowers should never compete in importance with the painting but should lead the eye to it by design, and emphasize it by color relationship.

I have a friend who has an original watercolor landscape in fall colors hanging over an antique desk. On the top of the desk is an antique mahogany cheese tray like the one in Plate 1. Some of the time the cheese tray is just filled to overflowing with yellow, green, brown, and orange gourds, which accent the colors in the picture. But on gala occasions she does a really breathtaking arrangement in this container, keeping the flowers low in the center, but following the flaring sides with sweeping curves that frame the lower part of the painting. I will never forget one that was a combination of cream stock, yellow carnations, talisman roses, russet and gold chrysanthemums, gray-green eucalyptus foliage, elderberry, with a few apples, grapes, and kumquats at the center focal point.

It is fun to do unexpected arrangements in the living room. On a fall day, try putting a brass kettle full of bright-colored red, gold, cream, and yellow zinnias on a brass trivet inside the fireplace opening. Or on Hallowe'en putting a lighted jack-o'-lantern there. Make an arrangement inside a globular apothecary jar. Or fill a large fluted giant clamshell with a rooting medium and plant cuttings in it for a corner near a window. Another amusing and attractive thing to do is to turn a tip-top table so that the pedestal top is exposed, and use it as a base for a flower arrangement whose background is the tilted tabletop.

In the living rooms of modern houses, it is particularly important to consider the dimensional quality in arrangements, for they are often placed against glass walls, or on the shelves of room dividers where they are seen from both sides. Because there is a transition from indoors to outdoors in these houses, natural containers like roots, stumps, and driftwood are particularly suitable. This doesn't mean that the container has to be rough. The wood can be peeled, waxed, and polished so that it has a finish compatible with the finest furniture. Containers of metal or fine pottery are also good, as are Oriental containers of metal or bamboo. The arrangement in Fig. 26 is appropriate for a modern house.

A woman that I know who has such a house found a huge piece of narrow bark one day, in the form of a perfect crescent. She made it the basis of a stunning arrangement, by fastening the crescent to a base of rough wood, which in turn she put on a piece of flagstone. She followed the inner curve of the crescent with three aspidistra leaves, and put three shaggy orange dahlias at the focal point. This arrangement was equally beautiful from either side.

Arrangement by Myra Brooks

Figure 26. A stunning arrangement that can be assembled from a "collector's shelf," of palm, dried artichoke, yucca pods, embryo palm, and a root. (Photo by Roche)

Arrangements in these houses should be bold and dramatic in design. Foliage colors are admirably suited to these houses, because of the muted and outdoor colors often used in their decoration. But when flowers are used, they can be bold also in form and color. Good ones to use are anthuriums, bird-of-paradise, day lilies, gladiolus, calla lilies, ginger, and poker plants.

ARRANGEMENTS FOR
THE DINING ROOM

Principles of Setting a Table

ONE OF the most creative tasks in the daily household chores of a woman is to set a table. Whether it is a bride's dinner for two on a card table or a family dinner for ten in a dining room, it takes only a little imagination and ingenuity to have different effects. If you realize this, and become interested, you will find yourself searching through remnant counters for fabrics to make cloths or place mats. You will use things you never thought of as table linen—chintzes, cretonnes, upholstery fabric, felt. You will find unusual objects around the house that you can use in a centerpiece with flowers, fruit, or foliage, or even sometimes by themselves, to make your table original and different.

Instead of dreading the routine chore, you will find yourself thinking, "We're having fish tonight. I think I'll cover that sea-green cloth with a fishnet, and bring in those colored glass Japanese fishing balls from the porch to use in the center of the table." Or, "We're having Italian spaghetti and red wine tonight. I think I'll use straw-covered wine bottles for candlesticks and a wicker tray of grapes for a centerpiece."

There are many things that govern a table setting. How many people are to be served? Is it seated or buffet? Where is the table— kitchen, dining room, patio, or terrace? Is it for breakfast, luncheon, or dinner? Is it a party or a family meal?

The size of the table, and how many are to be served, is the first thing to consider. If a table seats four or six, and four or six are to be served, the meal would probably be seated. If there are eight or more people, it would be buffet.

For a seated meal, the table accessories, china, glass, and silver are placed the same, whether the meal is breakfast, lunch, or dinner. The centerpiece can be in the middle of the table, with each place setting equidistant around it, or it can be at one end, with the place settings along each side. If it is in the middle, it must be low enough so that people can easily see across it. If candles are used, the flame should never be at eye level.

Plates are placed equidistant from each other, with forks at the left of the plate, and knives and spoons at the right. The water glass goes on the right, above the tip of the knife, and butter plates and napkins at the left. Whether the corners of the napkin point toward the plate or away from it is a matter of personal preference. Salts and peppers are usually placed either side of the centerpiece on a small table, and at regular intervals on a larger one.

For a buffet table, the centerpiece is usually placed at the back, if the table is against a wall, or in the middle if the table is in the center of the room. There is really no set rule where it must be on a buffet table, as its placement is balanced by the other serving appointments that are on the table. On a buffet table the knives and forks are placed altogether as part of the whole design of the table, as are the plates, napkins, and serving dishes.

The cloth is the background for a table setting. I use the word "cloth" loosely, because you could also use the bare polished wood tabletop, a glass-topped table, or mats of various kinds. Soft colors are easiest to work with, although it is fun sometimes to accept the challenge of a brilliant color. Do have as many different colored cloths as you can. You may not have a great variety of china or patterns of glass, but with different color combinations in table linens and flowers, it is easy to change the whole effect of your table.

This doesn't necessarily mean a big investment. If you have white damask cloths left from your trousseau (or your mother's) get them out and dye them. They dye beautifully. You can pick up damask cloths at many auctions for a song. Old-fashioned heavy linen sheets, cut in a circle and dyed, make charming circular cloths. And as we said before—there are always the remnant counters.

Many people have gold and white china. How much more interesting it is, instead of always using it with a white cloth, to plan different color schemes. You can put it on a damask cloth dyed a soft green, and have a centerpiece of yellow acacia and daffodils, or you could use a cloth of dull gold linen with a centerpiece of daisies and yellow privet.

If blue is your favorite color, plan to use your blue cloths for luncheon, as this color "fades" in artificial light. If your china is decorated with blue, use warm colors with it at night. I am thinking of a woman whose favorite plates are cream-colored pottery with a circle of Wedgwood-blue grapes and vines embossed on the edge. For lunch they are lovely on pale blue mats with a centerpiece of forget-me-nots, violets, and heather. At night this would be very dull. Instead, she uses them on a pale pink cloth with deep violet goblets, and a centerpiece of heather, pink carnations, pink sweet peas, blue grape hyacinths, and purple anemones, and the table sings.

You don't have to have expensive china and glass to have beautiful tables. Fortunately the shops are full of this merchandise with moderate prices and good design. The latter is most important.

We think of the whole table as one design. As in a flower arrangement each part should relate to the whole in color, scale, texture, and suitability. The table, too, should be in keeping with the room in which it is set, so that it blends with the other furnishings in color and quality.

There are several questions that always arise in discussions of table settings. One is, "Can you use table mats at dinner?" There is no rule that says you can't. Solid backgrounds are usually used at dinner for the common-sense reason that it is more restful to see an unbroken background than the divided area made by mats, and at night people are apt to be tired. Another question is, "Can you use candles at luncheon?" It is generally considered better not to have candles at any meal before dusk. After all—why have them? They aren't needed for light, and if you want them for color, there are other ways to introduce it.

The third question frequently asked, stems from the true statement that at a seated table the flower arrangement should be low enough so that it doesn't obstruct the view of people seated opposite each other. It is very disconcerting to have to peek around a bowl of flowers to talk to a person on the opposite side of the table. People ask, "If you are using a large container like a soup tureen or a large bowl, don't the flowers have to be tall to be in good proportion to the container?" The answer to this is, "Keep the

STEP-BY-STEP ARRANGEMENT

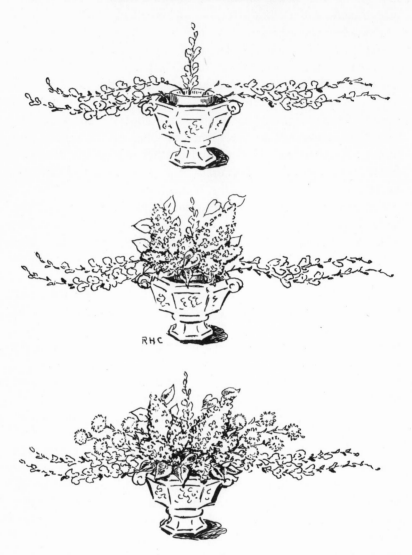

flowers short in height, but extend them at the sides so that you have horizontal proportion instead of vertical." A good example of this is the arrangement of gladiolus in a glass bowl in Plate 10. Flowers with a spiky form such as snapdragon, heather, astilbe, gladiolus, stock, delphinium, and annual larkspur are good for making the outline of this type of arrangement. If you don't have spiky flowers, you can use foliage like iris leaves, huckleberry, leucothoe, and laurel to get the same effect.

The way to go about making a long, low arrangement for the center of a dining table is illustrated in the step-by-step drawings on page 162. Put whatever you are using for mechanics—needle-holder or Oasis—in the container. Then put a spiky-form flower in the center, extending approximately twelve inches above the container. Next put a longer spiky form extending out each side. You have now established a triangular design, with a horizontal hypotenuse. Complete the side of the arrangement facing you. This is less confusing than if you keep turning the container around and around as you work.

Fill in the outline with other flower forms and foliage, using buds at the outside edge, and shorter spiky forms to support the original lines. Next, establish a focal point at the center. Now turn the container around, and do the other side in the same manner. The two sides don't have to be identical in placement of the flowers. In fact it is more interesting, although the same color scheme should prevail, to have a completely different focal point in color and form on each side. In an arrangement in shades of lavender, pink, rose, and purple, you could have pink roses at the focal point on one side, and purple pansies on the other. For a finishing touch to the arrangement, turn each end toward you, and fill in any place at the side that seems necessary.

An exception to the rule of keeping low the flowers in the center of the table is the use of a tall flowering branch or a piece of driftwood, with flowers at the base. The view is then not obstructed since you can see through the branches.

Any plant material used on a table must be in very good condition. Flowers must be fresh and foliage clean. Any damaged leaves should be removed. Fruit should be polished and free of blemishes. Think how unappetizing it would be to sit down at the table and be confronted with worm holes!

In the busy lives that most of us lead, a leisurely breakfast seems to be impractical. That is why it is nice to make an occasion of the times when the family can be together at the breakfast table on a weekend, a holiday morning, or when there are guests. Because it may be infrequent, a leisurely breakfast at a prettily set table seems like a special treat.

Breakfast Tables and Breakfast Trays

A breakfast table should be cheerful and have a "wake up" feeling. China, glasses, and linen should be sparkling clean and colors bright. This is a time to use informal and gay table settings. In an Early American house, for instance, yellow Quimper pottery plates, with their touches of dark green, dark blue, and orange would be pretty on a green cloth. For a centerpiece you might use two painted wooden peasant figures, to relate to the ones on the plates, standing by a low arrangement of lemons, limes, kumquats, and dark blue grapes.

Or you could start with a figurine suggesting early morning sounds, like ceramic roosters, birds, or (where I live) ducks, and build the table setting around them. You could put white ceramic roosters on either side of a circle of white eggcups filled with sprigs of red begonia and use white pottery plates on a red cloth. Or, you might choose straw place mats, green plates with a pattern of daisies, green glasses, and a straw basket of daisies for a centerpiece.

In a more formal house, china like the well-known "moss rose" pattern would be pretty on pink linen place mats with a bowl of just-picked fragrant garden roses for a centerpiece. Or white plates with a soft gray-green border on cloth of the same color, with a milk glass basket filled with spicy white garden pinks and their gray-green foliage as a centerpiece, would make a cool, refreshing way to start a hot summer's day.

Even on the busy mornings, when breakfast may be a hurried one at the kitchen counter bar, a copper coffeepot full of marigolds at the end, echoing the color in the orange-juice glasses, would make the morning seem more cheerful, or a freshly picked bunch of mint in a tall sugar shaker would add its fragrance to that of brewing coffee.

Sometimes it is fun to pamper someone and take him breakfast on a tray. If you do, plan the tray appointments as carefully as though you are setting a table. Be sure that it has all the necessary china, silver, and other things like cream, sugar, salt and pepper, and make a little arrangement for it. This should be in something that won't tip over easily. You could use pansies in a small brown luster pitcher, Johnny-jump-ups in a little pewter sugar bowl, or you might snip two or three white cyclamen blossoms with a few of their leaves and put them in a child's silver mug. A newly opened rose, with the dew still on it, in a bud vase would make a lovely way to say, "Good morning."

Invalids need trays at times other than breakfast, and it can give them great pleasure if there is a different little nosegay on each tray. It is nice to make these fragrant. A few lilies of the valley and violets in a silver pepper shaker, some garden pinks in a pressed-glass toothpick holder, or some sprigs of mock orange in a gold and white demitasse cup can do wonders to perk up drooping spirits.

In planning a luncheon or a dinner table setting, the first thing to consider is your dining room, for the period of the furnishings and the color and texture of the draperies and rugs and wallpaper will form the background for the table. You can easily see that if your furniture is eighteenth-century mahogany, and the draperies and wallpaper are in shades of pink, rose, and deep red, no matter how much you might want to set a table with yellow majolica pottery and a centerpiece of marigolds the result would not be harmonious. Or, if you wanted to use an heirloom lace cloth, and your table is in a family-style kitchen dining room, it wouldn't be appropriate.

Luncheon and Dinner Tables

You would naturally use a color scheme for the table that would blend with the one already in the room. In most dining rooms there is a wide enough color range so that you can have plenty of variation. You can choose one of the colors in the draperies, for instance, for the main color and pick up other colors in the room for contrast or accent, varying the main color at different times. Or you can choose one color in the room and do a monochromatic table setting, using different shades of one color.

While the different parts of the table setting don't have to be authentic, it does give a greater feeling of unity if, in an Early American, an eighteenth-century, a Victorian, or a modern house, the table as a whole suggests the period.

In many houses built within recent years, a dining room as such has been eliminated, and a dining area is incorporated as part of a family kitchen, or an alcove in the living room. If the kitchen dining room is furnished with sturdy comfortable furniture, pine-paneled or painted walls, table settings appropriate for an Early American house would be suitable. However, in some houses the dining area of a kitchen has glass walls, a floor or window garden of plants, and quite formal wrought-iron furniture. In this case, more elegant table settings would be proper. In a dining alcove that is a part of a living room, the furnishings of the living room would be the key to the table setting.

In every discussion of luncheon and dinner tables the question arises, "What is the difference between formal and informal?" This is not an easy question to answer, because there are actually no set rules. Rather, it is a quality that you feel.

Informal settings are gay. They can have a feeling of amusement. There is a relaxed feeling to an informal table. Figurines, used with the centerpiece, may set a mood or tell a story.

Formal tables, on the other hand, have a quality of elegant simplicity. Without being ornate, they look "dressed up." Flower arrangements are usually in more conventional-type containers. Napkins are larger. Crystal goblets are used instead of tumblers. Added pieces such as service plates and finger bowls may be used.

The cost of the table appointments is not the criterion. Let's for fun see what would be the difference between a formal and an informal dinner table in an eighteenth-century-type dining room. The background, of course, is the same for both tables.

For the informal dinner table the cloth could be pale pink linen. The china would have a border design of flowers in shades of pink and rose. The goblets would be heavy, in a simple tulip shape. The centerpiece could be branches of pink flowering quince, with deep rose-red foliage hiding the cup pinholder, placed at one end of a piece of fine white marble. Two Boehme birds could be placed at the other end to carry out the line of the branches.

In the same room, using the same china and silver, for the formal dinner you could use a delicate fine linen and lace tablecloth, goblets of thinner crystal in a tapered shape, and for the centerpiece a silver epergne filled with roses, bleeding hearts, violets, and delphiniums.

The appointments for both tables are of fine quality and expensive. The difference is that the informal table is more colorful, gayer, and less elegant.

In an Early American house, for an informal table you could have green and white Wedgwood pottery on green linen place mats on a pine table. The glasses could be green goblets. The centerpiece could be a coffee grinder with red geraniums and leaves in the top, and red crab apples and green grapes spilling out the open drawer of the grinder onto the table.

For a formal table in the same house, the mats could be replaced by a heavy dark green cloth, the plates could be the same, the green goblets replaced by pewter ones, and the centerpiece a 'long low arrangement of white snapdragons, red geraniums, and green grapes in a pewter bowl.

Although in many ways table settings for luncheon and dinner are similar, there are some definite differences. One is color. As natural light is strongest at noon, luncheon is a time when you can use colors that lose their intensity under artificial light—blues, lavenders, and gray. Another difference is scale. Luncheon plates are smaller than dinner plates and luncheon napkins are smaller than dinner ones. While tumblers are used at luncheon, taller goblets are usually used for dinner. Since it is assumed that there is plenty of light at midday, candles are not used for luncheon, but they make a most flattering light to use at dinner. Although it is perfectly permissible to use them for dinner, table mats are more frequently used for luncheon.

Since most people own more tablecloths and types of glassware than they do patterns of china, it is the latter that is often the starting point for planning a table setting. There are certain kinds of china that many people have. One is the white china with a gold band of varying widths. This can be very handsome on a white damask cloth—but how about using a yellow one, with an arrangement of yellow hyacinths, yellow tulips, and forsythia, and brown beech leaves? Or try a deep green cloth with a gold and white antique bowl-shaped compote filled with yellow roses and their glossy dark green foliage, with green grapes spilling over the edge. Buttercups and daisies, although wildflowers, are so dainty and have such a satiny texture to their petals that they are a good choice to use with this china.

Then there is the dark blue and white pattern of Canton or Willow. There is nothing wrong with using either of these on a white cloth, but how much more interesting it would be to use a deep red cloth, with a centerpiece of pine branches accented by two or three large red dahlias and their buds in a shallow Oriental container. Or you could use either of these patterns with a pale pink cloth, with a centerpiece of budded camellia foliage and deep pink and rose blossoms in a low bowl. Or you could use them on a polished tabletop without a cloth, with a centerpiece of Japanese cherry branches in a rectangular copper container.

Probably the type of china that gives the most variety of color to work with is one with a floral pattern that combines many colors, like the one used on the buffet table in Plate 3. Here you can make any one of them the main color, and use the others in smaller or greater amounts for many different combinations.

Plain-colored pottery plates, like those of Russel Wright design, in green, white, black, yellow, or brown, are wonderful to use in modern houses and are stimulating to the imagination for different effects. Black plates on a shocking-pink cloth, with a centerpiece of pink anthurium placed in a cup pinholder on an Oriental black scroll stand, the pinholder hidden by lumps of coal would be stunning. With this combination you could use black Bennington pottery mugs instead of cups.

Brown plates on an orange cloth, with a centerpiece of yellow and orange poker plant and brown magnolia leaves, would be an inviting table setting on a cold day, while deep green ones on a white cloth, with a centerpiece of large grooved green hosta leaves and white carnations would be refreshing and cool-looking on a hot summer one.

When you set a luncheon or a dinner table on a terrace or patio, it is necessary to consider the wind. Table appointments should not be fragile. The centerpiece must be such that it won't blow over. If candles are used at dinner, they must be protected so that they won't blow out or drip all over the table.

It is fun to do tables out of doors, because the surrounding landscape is your background, and you aren't limited as to color, texture, and period. When I did the outdoor terrace table pictured in Plate 9 the idea started with an unusual coral fan that I found in Bermuda. When I brought it home, I didn't know what I would do with it, but I was intrigued with its dimensional quality and the way part of it curved around like a sail bellying in the wind. When I was thinking about the table, I remembered the fan and also that I had a coconut spathe that would be a natural for a "boat." The spathe wouldn't rest squarely on the table, so on the beach I found a piece of driftwood, smoothed the edges and fastened the spathe to it with Stickum. I also used Stickum to fasten the fan to the boat, and the base to the tablecloth. Now I was sure that my arrangement would not blow over.

An arching spray of miniature pink cymbidium orchids from a neighboring grower and a few leaves from a houseplant made the "passengers." I had a pink linen cloth, and some smoky purple pebbly glasses that related to the colors in the sea fan. When I found the shell-shaped crinkly glass plates in the same purple and pink colors in a gift shop, I remembered some oyster shells we had picked up on a fishing dock in Baltimore, thinking they would be nice to use for seafood cocktail. I got them out, scrubbed them well, and my table was set.

When I use this setting at night, I put the boat arrangement at one side of the center. On the other side I have an arrangement of candles. I found a piece of silvery gnarled driftwood in a rocker shape. My husband drilled holes in it at intervals to hold candles and surrounded it at the sides and back with a tall curved piece of transparent plastic to shield the candles from the prevailing wind.

One way to have flower arrangements on a terrace table that won't blow apart is to make flower arrangements inside the chimneys of tall hurricane lamps. One unusual one that I saw was done with tall spikes of horsechestnut blossoms inside each glass, and a low arrangement of the blossoms on the table between the lamps. The transition from the flowers inside to the ones outside was done with clematis vine in a graceful continuous line.

For an outdoor buffet barbecue table on a brick terrace, you could have a large dark green casserole of creamed potatoes or other hot dish to go with your grilled steak or hamburgers at one end of a harvest table, a large green pitcher of iced tea with green glasses at the other, and a row of red geraniums in their pots lined up across the back. (You could plant the geraniums after the party was over.)

Buffet Tables

A buffet-type setting for a table may be used for any meal—breakfast, luncheon, and dinner, and also for teas, cocktail parties, and other entertaining. It is an intriguing problem in design, for in addition to a flower arrangement you also have to place silver, china, napkins, serving dishes, and, if it is in the evening, candles.

The design must have good balance, and the different parts should be related in color, form, and texture. Because there are so many different objects to place in relation to each other, it is more difficult to set a buffet table artistically than one at which people are seated and where the place settings are symmetrical. Also, while the food for a seated dinner may be served by a waitress, or from a serving table, the food is a part of the design on a buffet table. At a flower show, in a class for buffet tables, the judges consider all these things, and many times, in a close decision between two tables, the ribbon goes to the one that has the greatest number of objects placed with the best effect.

An arrangement on a buffet table is usually at the back or at the side of the table. Its height is restricted only by its relation to the rest of the table. The arrangement in Fig. 27 could be used on a buffet table.

The color scheme for the buffet supper table in Plate 3 was suggested by the floral design on the white china, in which there was blue, lavender, yellow, and coral. Because the hostess wanted to use a pewter candelabrum, she chose pewter serving pieces and used dull stainless steel flatware instead of silver. She chose a lavender cloth because it emphasized the more subtle coloring in the china and was a good contrast with the soft gray of the pewter. For a flower container she used a pewter hexagonal-shaped sugar bowl, and selected flowers to repeat the colors in the china and cloth—lavender heather, purple anemone, yellow and white freesia, yellow acacia, blue iris, and coral azalea. Note that the pewter flower container is related in design to the salt and pepper shakers, which in turn relate in design to the candelabrum. The candelabrum is placed off-center to balance the visual weight of the flowers.

Let's see how to work out the problems of a buffet table by setting a hypothetical one. Suppose you have some plates and cups and saucers of highly glazed dark green pottery in a modern streamlined design. This means that the table will be one suitable for a modern house. You also have a handsome brass samovar which you want to use, which would be suitable in its bold design for a table of this type. You look for a cloth and find one in chartreuse linen bound in dark green, which seems perfect, as it is heavy enough in texture to go with the bold plates, and in color is a good tie-in between the green of the plates and the brass of the samovar. Your sister has four heavy brass candlesticks which you borrow.

Now comes the time to plan the placement of the different things, and what you will use for an arrangement. The samovar is large, and heavy both visually and physically, so your first thought

Arrangement by Myra Brooks

Figure 27. A gay arrangement using the primary colors of red carnations, red spotted rubrum lilies, yellow daffodils, and blue irises. Notice that the use of two bases gives stability and distinction. (Photo by Roche)

is that to have good balance on the table the samovar should be at the back in the center. "But then," you think, "the candlesticks will have to go at one end, and the arrangement at the other. They will then have to equal each other in visual weight, and since the candlesticks aren't nearly as heavy visually as the samovar, it will be too dominant in the center of the table."

You see, then, that it would be better to put the samovar at one end and make the arrangement heavy enough to equal it at the other. The candlesticks can be lined up across the back and balanced by the serving pieces in front of them.

Now—what will we use for the arrangement? It must be heavy enough to equal the samovar in visual weight. There must be glossy texture to relate to the shiny brass and the high glaze of the pottery. The container and plant material must be suitable for heavy liner pottery, and brass. The colors should incorporate green, chartreuse, brassy yellow, and a contrasting color for accent.

Why not choose a fruit, vegetable, and foliage arrangement? It would be heavy and suitable for the other table appointments. You could arrange it in a shallow brass-footed bowl. The fruit and vegetables would include a highly polished eggplant (good color contrast, texture, and form for height), green pears, yellow plums, green limes, and green and purple grapes. For foliage you could use green glossy camellia foliage and chartreuse leucothoe. You can see how this arrangement would balance the table and tie it together in color and texture.

But we aren't through yet. We must think of food and serving pieces. The cups and saucers can be placed diagonally in front of the samovar. To balance this design, a salad bowl (perhaps one of the crinkly yellow-green pottery ones in the shape of an opened cabbage) could go on the arrangement end of the table, with the flatware and napkins placed diagonally in front of it. In the center of the table, in front of the candlesticks, giving added weight there, you could put a large dark green casserole on a brass tray.

Sometimes there are so many objects to go on a buffet table that there is little room for a flower arrangement. One way to solve this is to use a candelabrum, and combine candles and plant material. There are several mechanical ways to do this. In the market now, sold at florists' shops, are small glass bowls with a little projection at the bottom that fits in a candlestick. You can use one of these bowls filled with flowers in the center of a candelabrum, the candles in the other holders, for an evening buffet. For a luncheon buffet you can use the bowls in all the candlesticks of a candelabrum and have flowers in each, making a very unusual container. Or, for a seated dinner table, you can put one in a low candlestick, which makes a footed container suitable for a long, low centerpiece.

There is also another glass container on the market to use with a candlestick or candelabrum, a hollow glass ring that surrounds the base of a candle. These are fun to use, because you can make charming arrangements with "bits and pieces" of plant material. The containers are so shallow that what you really do is fashion small wreaths, using the heads of small flowers, tiny buds, and leaves, around the base of the candle. Mechanics are unnecessary because the flowers are so close together that they support themselves.

If you don't have, or can't get, the glass containers, you can still have the same effect by using Oasis. Soak a two- or three-inch cube of Oasis and wrap it in green foil or plastic, tying it firmly like a package with heavy thread. (The wrapping is to make sure no water will drip on the tablecloth.) Take two wires about fifteen inches long and insert them at right angles through the center of the Oasis. Place the packaged Oasis on top of the empty candle-holder and fasten it there by winding the ends of the wire around and around it.

In the Oasis you can make an unusual and attractive arrangement with a mere handful of flowers. Establish a design by placing a short spiky flower in the center, and another at each side. Fill in toward the center with round forms, concealing the Oasis. (If the plastic covering is tough, and you have trouble inserting the stems, you can prepare the way by making a small hole with a nail or other sharp object.) Spiky flowers that are nice to use are the tips or sidepieces of delphiniums or annual larkspurs, side shoots of heather, or buds of spray chrysanthemums. Don't be afraid to cut the stems short—you have to keep the arrangement in scale, for it must look like part of the candelabrum unit. You can use the larger flowers of a spray of chrysanthemums or clusters of florets from the base of stock, delphinium, and snapdragon stalks to fill in the center. Flowers with round forms, small enough in scale, and with stems sturdy enough to stick in the Oasis are sweet peas, tiny roses, daisies, nicotiana, and stephanotis.

Fruits used with a candelabrum make an interesting centerpiece. Think of the candelabrum and the fruit as one arrangement, with the candles as the high point. The candelabrum should be placed on a base—a pewter plate, mahogany board, a mirror or a small silver tray turned upside down. Arrange some fruit selected according to the color scheme you want, on the base, at each side of the candelabrum. The scale of the fruit should be small. Seckel pears, lady apples, kumquats, crab apples, strawberries, plum, cranberries, clusters of cherries, small limes, and small green grapes are all suitable. Make the transition from the fruit arrangement at the base to the candles with sprays of berried vines winding up the candelabrum. Cotoneaster with coral berries, fire thorn with orange, viburnum with purplish black, bayberry with pewter, pokeweed with purplish black, juniper with blue, bittersweet with red and orange, and rose-colored rose hips are just some of the berries in the color range available. Vines to use with them could be clematis, small curly ivy, tradescantia, and grape ivy.

Impromptu and Winter Arrangements for Tables

Someone who lives in New England once said to me, "What can you do for a table centerpiece in that time between Christmas and Easter when there are no garden flowers and they are so expensive to buy in the shops?"

There are a number of things to do, but it does require more ingenuity and imagination. This is a time to look around the house and find something you are using as decoration in a part of the house other than the dining room. Perhaps with the addition of very little live plant material it will make a pleasing centerpiece.

You may have one of those antique latticework china compotes on a living room table. You could fill it with some of the luscious-looking artificial lemons and green grapes that are available, add some real limes (artificial ones never seem to have the natural rich coloring) and some clusters of laurel from the dooryard, or sprigs of ivy geranium from a houseplant in water picks. With a pair of Sheffield grape scissors thrust in the top, it wouldn't occur to most people that this arrangement isn't all live.

In the library, there may be a wooden duck decoy. Bring him to the table, and let him nestle under an arrangement of dried grasses from the field. If you have a copper tray, use some leaves like aspidistra or bird's-nest fern for height in an arrangement on it, and for flower forms the ruffled round geranium leaves whose edges are ringed with bronze. Some chunks of brown glass used with this would be a distinctive accent. You can use branches with a sculptured form like manzanita or driftwood, and for flowers with them, wood roses or coconut calyxes from your dried flower box.

If you have houseplants, you can make a very colorful bouquet in one of the Oasis holders described in Part I under "Mechanical Aids" by stretching out the horizontal line with grape ivy, tradescantia, laurel, or ivy, and using snips of begonia, kalanchoe, African violet, azalea, fuchsia, or cineraria for color in the center.

A succession of paper-white narcissus bulbs planted at intervals in low flat containers and brought out at the height of their bloom will give you flowers over a long period. For a more colorful centerpiece you can buy some croton leaves, which will last a long time. You can use them alone, changing the color scheme of the other table appointments to emphasize one of the many colors in the leaves, or combine them with greens or accessories like colored glass, a figurine, or a piece of sculpture. And then, last but not least, there are always forced branches.

At dinnertime you can use the glass bowls with a candelabrum or candlesticks, as described under "Buffet Tables," or you can get one of the many interesting large chunky candles that are available, put it on a board, tray, or mirror, and make an arrangement of greens, fruit, or vegetables around it.

An allied problem in table setting is that of the impromptu or last-minute arrangement. Probably all of us have had the experience of having unexpected guests for lunch or dinner when there isn't a trace of a flower on the dining table.

Just as you have cans of food for a meal for such unexpected guests on an emergency shelf, you should be prepared also for quick and impromptu table arrangements. Some day when your hands are occupied with sewing or knitting, and your mind is free, dream up some good ideas. Mentally catalogue the accessories you could use or containers that you can fix quickly. Be aware of any foliage that is available in the yard. Then when the time comes, you won't panic. You can whip up an arrangement in no time. Think how easily the composition in Fig. 28 could be assembled.

You might twine philodendron around the graceful figurine of the Chinese goddess from your living room mantel. Your plant could probably benefit from a little pruning anyway. Or rush out in the yard and cut a foliage bouquet. If, in the yard you have as few

Arrangement by Mrs. Raymond Wismer

Figure 28. An easily assembled composition using a single branch of cactus, some succulents, and two figurines on a base dusted with sand. (Photo by Roche)

as two or three daffodils or roses in bloom, cut them different lengths and put them with their foliage on a pinholder at one side of a shallow container, letting the water serve as part of the design. Take a pot of blooming African violets from a window sill and put them pot and all in a pretty bowl.

Go and look in the icebox. There might be a couple of artichokes and some green grapes. Put the artichokes in the center of a flat glass plate, lay the grapes across each side, and tuck in a few green leaves.

ARRANGEMENTS FOR BEDROOMS

FLOWERS can give just the needed finishing touch to a bedroom. In the picture in Fig. 29 the arrangements of ferns in handsome antique containers are an important decorative feature of an eighteenth-century bedroom.

The other day I went into a bedroom to leave my coat and was intrigued by an arrangement on a small table. The room was very feminine and the furniture was delicate and French. On a slender round-topped table were sprays of fragile-looking fern (the kind you often see garlanding a wedding cake) arranged in a most unusual container. I went closer to examine it and found that it was made by fastening two opaque white goblets base to base—probably with Stickum. It was just right for the room, and so unusual that, simple as it was, it was the first thing you noticed.

A glass perfume bottle seems a logical and beautiful container for a few sweet-smelling flowers—lilies of the valley, violets, or sweet peas—on a dressing table. There might be a silver baby shoe also on the dressing table, and what would be more fitting than to fill it with baby's breath?

If your bedroom is Victorian, perhaps you can find a pair of large perfume bottles—the kind with narrow necks and globular bottoms like the one pictured in Fig. 30. Arrangements in these of spicy rose geranium leaves with a few blossoms of white geranium at the focal point would be lovely on either end of a wide mahogany chest. (You could use real foliage and artificial flowers for a long-lasting arrangement.)

There is a particular shade of dusty rose-pink that is often

Figure 29. Delicate brake and hare's-foot fern, planted in antique containers, add an elegant note to an eighteenth-century bedroom. (Photo by Roche)

found in bedroom chintzes. In the fall the perfect thing to use in an arrangement for a bedroom that has this color is abelia. This is a shrub with small evergreen leaves, and during the summer it has a small white bell-shaped flower. In the fall when the flowers fall off, a cluster of bracts is left, which look like small flowers, and are this exact dusty rose color.

Once when I was visiting in the South, every morning on my dressing table there was a little triangular mound of fresh hibiscus flowers placed under the mirror. This would be nice to do in the bedroom of a modern house. If you live in the North and don't have hibiscus, you could do the same thing with mallows or day lilies.

A child will be fascinated to have in his bedroom a dish garden

Arrangement by Katherine N. Cutler

Figure 30. White geraniums are related in color and texture to an antique cologne bottle. (Photo by Roche)

with small succulents and cacti arranged for artistic effect. These are among the easiest of plants to grow and require little care. Can you imagine his interest if his plants are named peppermint stick, tiger jaws, necklace vine, fairy washboard, tiny Tim, pony tail, or baseball plant? These are all listed in catalogues. He can add sand and flat stones to have it resemble a Western landscape, and to make it even more realistic he can add tiny cowboys and Indians.

It is nice to think of fragrance for a bedroom when you are planning outside planting. No one who has slept in a first-floor bedroom with a bank of rose geraniums under the window or in a second-floor room with lilac blossoms touching the window sill will ever forget the wonderful scent on the night air.

ARRANGEMENTS FOR KITCHENS

IT IS more than just coincidence that in almost every picture you see of a model kitchen in a magazine there is an arrangement of flowers, fruit, or vegetables, or a thriving plant. The competent decorators who plan the layouts know that this plant material adds greatly to the charm of the room. In these days when so many houses are servantless, it is important to make the kitchen as attractive as any other room, for a family spends much of its time there.

In my kitchen the thing that gives me the most pleasure is a lucky accident. I have a corner sink, and the corner is formed by two picture windows which look out on a field full of bayberry, juniper, native shrubs, willow trees, and the water of Barnegat Bay. Since this makes a natural landscape background, I thought the triangle formed by the right-angled windows above the sink would be an ideal place for flowering plants. I wanted a tray to fit it to hold pebbles to put the plants on, and my husband, who at that time was putting a Fiberglas bottom on his boat, made me one of wood, two inches deep, and coated it, like the boat, with Fiberglas.

Sad to say, it was not a success for plants, because the angles were so sharp that pots fitted only in the very center, leaving gaping spaces at the corners. I tried different-sized pots with no success, and finally in disgust I threw the tray in the trash barrel. My husband found it there and, naturally resenting such treatment of his handiwork, rescued it and brought it back. I was a bit remorseful, and so started thinking of ways to use it. I hit on the idea, since the Fiberglas is completely waterproof, of using it as a large flower

container. Since then it has been my pride and joy and a conversation piece for everyone who sees it.

In November and December I keep it full of paper-white narcissus. To hold the bulbs I use pieces of stone that I have collected in different places. As I stand at the sink on a bitterly cold day, I look at the pink granite and am transported to the ancient ruins of the pilgrimage city of Baalbek, high on a Lebanon plain. The smooth round marble pebbles make me see again the deserted island of Delos, its surface covered with an Oriental carpet of bright-colored wildflowers among the marble ruins of a city surrounding the mythical birthplace of Apollo. The warm beige-colored sandstone brings a picture of the inscrutable Sphinx and the solid pyramids, standing golden against a vivid blue sky, and the pieces of eroded coral take me in memory to the aquamarine water and pink beaches of Bermuda. The fragrance of the narcissus promises that spring will come.

When the first daffodils come in the shops, I put away the rocks, scrub out the tray and fill it with water. I buy a dozen or so daffodils every week or ten days and make naturalistic clumps of the flowers, leaves, and buds, in different-sized pinholders scattered in the tray. Later on, in the very early spring, I put forced flowering branches in pinholders at the edges of the tray, as though they were arching over a pool, and nestle the first crocuses, grape hyacinths, or violets at their feet. In the summer I fill the tray with blocks of Oasis and make a miniature flower garden—sometimes one of foaming petunias and sometimes with mixed garden flowers.

For your kitchen, why not fasten an old-fashioned salt box to the wall, put a container to hold water in it, and fill it with a bouquet of fresh assorted herbs? Or put marigolds, fresh from the garden, in a black iron cooking pot?

Instead of putting a cabbage, some spinach, tomatoes, and green peppers in the refrigerator as soon as you come from the market, take a couple of minutes (and I mean literally that) to curl back some of the outer leaves of the cabbage so that it looks like a huge green rose, and put it on a breadboard with some of the tomatoes and green peppers piled against it. Clusters of the dark green spinach leaves will give grace to the arrangement. You can enjoy the rich color and form of the vegetables all day until it is time to prepare them for dinner.

If you have two baskets of fresh strawberries, their green hulls still intact, put one on each plate of a scale, tipping the baskets so that some of the berries spill out. They will contribute to the attractiveness of your kitchen all day and the berries will taste all the better at dessert that night for being at room temperature.

ARRANGEMENTS FOR BATHROOMS

FLOWERS in a bathroom? you say. Why not? Visitors to Japan, the cradle of the art of flower arrangement, are delighted to find flowers and plants not only in bathrooms, but in the public rest rooms of inns.

You naturally think of water in connection with a bathroom, and it is appropriate to use things associated with it. Wouldn't a lavabo fastened to the wall, the basin filled with ferns, be pretty? You could fasten a glass shelf to the wall and have a collection of vines rooted in water in small glass tumblers that match the color of your towels.

You might want to pick up the main color in your decorative scheme with a bouquet of flowers in an antique shaving mug on the counter—bachelor's buttons for blue, yellow chrysanthemums or marigolds for yellow, or rambler roses for pink.

On a window sill you might have a plant in a bottle. This is made like a terrarium but consists of only one plant that has a definite pattern, like a fern. The bottle could originally have held bath salts. Or, in a pastel-colored round box that once held bath powder, you could have a bouquet of pink and lavender clover and daisies.

One woman had a most original idea for her bathroom. She turned the top of the toilet tank (which was under a window with good light) upside down, and uses it for a tray. The tray is filled with pebbles, and on the pebbles are pots of African violets in bloom. The plants thrive in the light and humidity and are a mass of flowers.

PARTY ARRANGEMENTS

Teas ONE OF the most gracious of all parties is an afternoon tea. It is a lovely way to introduce a new daughter-in-law, entertain the visiting mother of a friend or neighbor, or honor a newly engaged girl. In these busy times with books, magazine articles, and radio broadcasts featuring time-saving short cuts for the daily routine of our lives, it is refreshing to turn the clock back once in a while to more leisurely days when tea in the afternoon was an accepted custom.

A tea party is the time to polish your silver service, unwrap your most delicate cloth, and get out your most fragile teacups. A tea table is set like a buffet table. The conventional arrangement is to have a tea service at one end of the table and a coffee service at the other. The flower arrangement is usually in the center, and unlike that for a dinner table can be as tall as you wish provided it is in proportion to the size of the table. This can be flanked by candlesticks or candelabra.

If the other furnishings in your house are in keeping, you can use a cloth of fine lace, delicately embroidered linen, a combination of linen and lace, or sheer organdy. One woman I know uses a beautiful mantilla of Spanish lace like a runner down the center of a highly polished mahogany table. If you want a touch of color, you can put a colored sheet under a sheer cloth.

With cloths like these, flower containers might be a silver or crystal bowl, a compote, an epergne, or an antique tureen. While an arrangement of one kind of flower like roses or lilies is lovely, it is a little more interesting to have mixed flowers in shades that blend with the colors in the room. You might use a combination

of lavender- and cream-colored stock, pink snapdragons, pink carnations, purple pansies, and deep red roses. Or for a different color
scheme, dark and light blue delphiniums, blue lace flowers, blue
irises with yellow centers, and yellow roses. For a table in a Victorian-type house you could use old-fashioned flowers—pansies,
fuchsia, marguerites, mignonettes, violets, and pinks in an epergne
or a silver cake basket.

If your house is furnished in sturdy pine or maple, and you
don't feel a dainty lace cloth or fragile cups are suitable, you can
still have a very dressy tea. Your cloth could be of embroidered
linen perhaps a little heavier than the ones mentioned above. You
could use pretty pottery like Wedgwood or Spode, or the less
elaborate patterns of fine china. You could also have your flowers
in a bowl, epergne, or tureen, but the bowl might be of pottery,
the epergne of milk glass, and the tureen of ironstone. You could
use for flowers a combination of white snapdragons, pink hyacinths, pink and white tulips, lavender ageratum. Or, for a different color scheme, cream-colored stock, yellow tulips, daffodils,
orange ranunculus, and bronze leucothoe.

Morning Coffees

Among many young married people, morning coffees have replaced afternoon teas. They are given for the same reasons as teas,
but the time is more sensible for young mothers, as they can
entertain and be entertained while children are in school in the
morning.

The table is buffet, the same as for a tea, but is more colorful
and less elegant. Cloths are usually colored, and the flower arrangements are less conventional. On a table with a brown cloth,
for instance, a copper scale would be a good choice for a container.

The bottom plate could have an arrangement of fruit—lemons,
kumquats, brown pears, and green figs. The upper plate might
have an arrangement of brown mahonia leaves and orange fire
thorn berries, with a few of the berries tucked in the fruit arrangement also.

On a pink cloth, an iron stove top filled with pink and rose
garden roses and gray dusty miller foliage would be attractive. Or,
since this party is in the morning, it would be an excellent time
to use a blue combination, if it fits the other things in the room,
and have a Canton tureen filled with bachelor's buttons and red
rambler roses on a blue cloth.

Birthdays

Next to Christmas the most important day in the life of a child is his birthday. And a birthday is a special day for a person of any age, whether he admits it or not. An older person may protest that it is a day to be ignored rather than celebrated, but I can't think of anyone who wouldn't be pleased, secretly or otherwise, to have some special attention on his birthday.

One charming birthday custom was brought back to us by a friend who was a major with the Military Government in Germany after the last world war. One day, walking through the bombed-out town where he was stationed, he felt sad. It was his birthday and he was a long way from his wife and children in America. The ruins in the town and the unhappy-looking people didn't help his feeling of depression. He walked wearily into the dining room where his fellow officers were gathered for dinner and noticed that his chair was missing from the table. As he started to look around for another, the door flew open, and in came two laughing maids carrying his chair. Everyone cried "Happy Birthday" as they put the chair at his place. And what a chair it was! It was completely outlined with flowers.

The two maids were Lithuanian, and when by chance they found out that it was the major's birthday they thought they would surprise him with one of the birthday customs of their country. They went into the fields and gathered flowers and leaves and fashioned garlands. These they fastened to the back, around the rungs, seat, and legs of the chair until it looked as though it was made of flowers instead of wood. This thoughtful attention couldn't have come at a more welcome time, and our friend was so pleased and impressed that he brought back the idea to all of us, and now his friends use the Lithuanian custom for birthdays in their families.

Flower garlands, like those used on the chair, are easy to make. Gather the flowers that you want to use the day before, so that they can be in water a long time before you use them. In addition to the flowers recommended in the section on Corsages, some of the sturdier wildflowers are good to use—daisies, black-eyed Susans, Queen Anne's lace. Cedar, juniper, laurel, huckleberry, and wild catbrier are good to use for greens.

When you make the garland, make little bunches of flowers with stems two to three inches long, and wire the stems together. As you make each bunch, put it in a container of water to keep fresh until you use it. When you have all the material assembled, make the garland as you would evergreen roping, as shown in the drawing on page 205. Fasten an end of heavy green twine or cotton rope to a doorknob or drawer handle to hold it taut while you are working. Start wiring the little bunches on the twine, making sure that the flowers overlap the stems of the preceding bunch. Wind round and round with a spool of wire in a continuous way. Put a little bunch of greens between every three or four bunches of flowers.

You might like to make a wreath for a "birthday girl" to wear at her party. To do this, wire tiny bunches of dainty flowers on a ribbon, leaving enough ribbon at each end so that you can tie the wreath around the head with a bow in the back. Or you can wire individual flowers as you would for a corsage. Make a circle to fit the head, of heavy wire or pliant wands of privet, willow, or forsythia from which you have stripped the leaves. Wind this with green florist's tape, and then wire the individual flowers on it.

We all know the lovely Hawaiian custom of greeting people with leis—garlands of flowers like long necklaces. Although in many parts of the country we don't have the ginger, frangipani, plumeria, and orchids with which these are made, there are many other things that can be used to make a lei for someone to wear on his birthday.

Use flowers that are rounded, like carnations, chrysanthemums, daisies, zinnias, and, with a needle and heavy thread, string the flower heads like beads, pushing each flower tightly against the one preceding it. Use one kind of flower for each lei. To keep the lei fresh, put it in a box lined with waxed paper, sprinkle it and put it in the refrigerator, or put it in a plastic bag with a little water sprinkled in it, in a cool place.

A birthday party wouldn't be complete without a cake, and you can have it double for a centerpiece. Use one that is baked in a pan with a hole in the center, like a sponge cake or an angel cake. Put it on a thin circle of Styrofoam cut a half inch wider all around than the circumference of the cake. Put the birthday candles in holders and stick them in the Styrofoam for a border around the bottom of the cake. In the hole at the top put a small glass, like a cheese glass, and fill it with dainty flowers. You can arrange more flowers and greens on the table to make a wreath around the base of the cake.

Some children (with a little help from their mother) recently planned a novel birthday table for their grandmother. Supper was an outdoor barbecue. When it was time for dessert, everyone came in the house. The children had put a winding garland (a rope of smilax bought from the florist) down the center of the table, and nestled along it like flowers were sixty cupcakes, each with a lighted candle. I don't know who was more excited, the children or the grandmother.

If a birthday falls near May Day, a pretty idea is to make a Maypole centerpiece. Stick a painted wooden dowel in a lump of florist's clay, or a piece of Styrofoam, and weave ribbons, as is done in a Maypole dance, a little way down from the top. Then draw the ends of the ribbons out to each place setting, and pin them to the tablecloth. You can put a little favor at the end of each ribbon and cover the base of the Maypole with flowers.

Children like birthday tables that are different. When my son was a cub scout, his birthday fell on the meeting day, so all the den members were invited for a birthday supper. I made a woodland setting in the center of the table, with moss, fern, seedling trees, bushes made from the tips of shrubs, and a small mirror pool. I found little animals in the proper scale, representing the different cub dens, and placed them around in the "woods." A group of the same animals was inside the circle of birthday candles around the rim of the cake. The boys thought it was great.

For a small child you might have a Peter Rabbit birthday table. You could use a piece of board or Styrofoam for a base, and on it make "Mr. McGregor's garden." You could make a cabbage patch with Brussels sprouts, and surround it on two sides with flowers and greens to make a shrubbery hedge. On the other two, you could make a fence with matchsticks. A figure of "Peter" and some miniature garden tools would complete the scene. Favors at each place could be sugar cookies in the shape of a rabbit, with a miniature watering can full of tiny flowers.

Or, you might have a "Three Little Kittens" table. Around the edges of a flat base, you could make a low shrubbery hedge, and in the center feature three toy kittens and a clothesline hung with six pink mittens. There could be a toy washtub filled with baby's breath to simulate soapsuds. A favor at each place could be a tiny ceramic kitten.

One of my young friends announced her engagement at a dinner party in a fun way. Paper cups, the proper size, were filled with a delicious mousse and placed in ordinary small flowerpots. The tops of the dessert were sprinkled with powdered chocolate to look like dirt, and a lovely rose with its foliage, its stem wrapped with foil at the bottom, was stuck in each pot as though it was growing there. The names of the young couple were written on garden tags and fastened to the roses. The exclamations that came when dessert was served were partly in surprise at the announcement, and partly for the pretty effect of the pots of roses. *Engagement Party*

Showers for engaged couples seem more imaginative these days than when they were largely limited to lingerie and kitchen utensils. *Showers*

One that is popular now is a wine shower. For the arrangement on the buffet table at such a party, you could put green wine bottles on graduated boards, and do line arrangements of grapevine in them. Put bunches of grapes on florist's picks and have them spilling from the necks of the bottles, and arrange other bunches on the boards. If you use natural grapevine it would be nice to use vine-ripened grapes. If it isn't the proper season for that, you could use grape ivy and grapes from the market.

Or if a wooden wine rack is to be one of the gifts, put it in the center of the table and trail vines across it (fastening them with Stickum) and have grapes spilling out of some of the openings in the rack. Make the effect lush, with the feeling of a vineyard. With this you could use candles in straw-covered wine bottles.

Another popular shower is the one where guests bring a favorite recipe on a file card, and a container of whatever ingredient makes the dish special. For the buffet table here, you could use a heavy linen cloth of brown or green, and make an arrangement of fresh herbs—artemisia, sage, rosemary, thyme, and mint in a green glazed pottery casserole.

For a bridesmaids' luncheon the table should be as pretty and feminine as possible. Use your daintiest linen, your thinnest glassware, and your prettiest china. You could have a cloth the color of the bridesmaids' dresses, and for a centerpiece make miniature replicas of their bouquets in smoke bells—the fluted white con- *Bridesmaids' Luncheon*

Arrangement by Myra Brooks

Figure 31. A frankly sentimental arrangement of hearts and flowers. Roses and carnations are combined with passionflower vine and hearts strung on a wire in a container supported by dancing cupids. (Photo by Roche)

tainers pictured in Plate 11. To do this, wedge a piece of soaked Oasis into the opening, and stick the flowers in this. Then put a single flower of the kind featured on each napkin.

On an occasion like this, where sentiment permits you to be "fancy," you could borrow an idea from the old-fashioned Jack Horner Pie for a centerpiece. Make an arrangement in the middle of the table of sentimental flowers like forget-me-nots, bleeding hearts, pansies, and lilies of the valley and have ribbons from the arrangement to each place. At the end of each ribbon, place the bridesmaid's present from the bride, prettily wrapped, with a spray of the flowers tied in the bow.

Or you might have a centerpiece like the one pictured in Fig. 31, using flowers similar to those the bridesmaids will carry.

IV
Holiday Arrangements

THANKSGIVING

AUTUMN is a time of blazing color, crisp invigorating air, and an abundance of Nature's bounty. Roadside stands are piled high with harvest fruits and vegetables, hard-shelled nuts fall to the ground in wooded groves, and country lanes are fragrant with the winy smell of wild grapes warmed in the sun. And just as the Pilgrims gathered three hundred years ago to give thanks for their first harvest, it is a time for family reunions and Thanksgiving.

Brilliant leaves, the last garden flowers, fruits, nuts, and vegetables make the most appropriate and beautiful decorations we can have for these festive dinner tables. Visit a roadside stand and arrangements for centerpieces will suggest themselves. A large silvery boat-shaped Hubbard squash just cries to be hollowed out and filled with the dark green acorn squash, green apples, red cabbage, purple cauliflower, and purple vine-ripened grapes surrounding it. Did you know that by carefully folding back the outside leaves of a red cabbage you can make it suggest a huge red rose? This, as well as acorn squash, can be impaled on heavy sticks to anchor them in the Hubbard squash arrangement. *Tables*

For a more formal table you can make an interesting fruit arrangement in a footed chalice container. Wedge a block of Oasis vertically in the opening, so that half of it is above the rim of the container. Use greens for the side and top lines of the arrangement. (Branches of juniper, loaded with gray-blue berries, are lovely at this time of year.) Fill in the center by wiring small fruits to florist's picks and sticking them in the Oasis, until it is completely covered. You could use cranberries on toothpicks in clusters, purple plums, tiny green pears, and bunches of green and purple grapes, the latter to hang over the edges.

Perhaps your china is white with a gold band, and you want to use a heavy white damask tablecloth. Why not use a garland as a centerpiece? This is particularly good for a large family table, because it is low enough not to interfere with any cross table conversation. You can lay flat magnolia or rhododendron leaves on the table in a garland pattern, or you can take small cuttings of ilex or boxwood and place them on the table so that they make a thick garland about five inches wide, or you can buy smilax roping from a florist. On the garland, put clusters of fruit at intervals, choosing those that are predominantly yellow and gold. You might have lady apples, kumquats, mandarins, Seckel pears, some tiny gourds, with some cranberries for accent.

If you are lucky enough to have an old silver epergne—the kind with a center container and smaller ones branching at the sides—this is the perfect time to use it. You can have either flowers or fruit in the center opening and make miniature fruit arrangements in the lower small ones. Be sure to choose fruits that are small in scale for the lower arrangements. Some of the lovely fall berries like viburnum, pokeweed, and fire thorn would fit in here.

Because of its association with harvest time, the cornucopia or "horn of plenty" is a suitable container for a Thanksgiving centerpiece. These are usually placed horizontally on the table and filled with fruit arranged so that some is spilling out on the table to typify harvest abundance. If you use a straw one, it would be especially nice to use wheat with the fruit—not only because wheat is appropriate to the season, but because it relates so well to the container in color and texture. When you use wheat, wire it into small sprays on a florist's pick. These are more effective in an arrangement than individual stalks.

An interesting centerpiece for a table in an Early American-type house would be nut trees. You make these with large pine cones, the ones that are seven or eight inches tall and five or six inches in diameter, with stiff open petals. Get a package of mixed nuts, walnuts, brazil nuts, pecans, almonds, and hazelnuts, and shellac them. When they are dry, put some glue on the end of each and thrust them between the petals of the pine cone. The result is a "tree" of interesting shape and colors—brown, mahogany, beige, and gold. Two or more of these in the center of the table, with some small chocolate turkeys clustered at the base, would be interesting and original.

If your dinner is to be in the evening, a very simple but effective centerpiece is to use grapes with candelabra. For a small table you would use only one, for a larger one, two. Fasten Oasis on the center cup as described in Part III under "Buffet Tables." Wire several bunches of grapes to florist's picks and insert them in the Oasis so that they hang down gracefully. Try and select a bunch that has a long stem curled in an interesting manner, so that you can fasten it across the top, with the stem making a definite line.

It is nice to have place cards for special dinners, and making them can be a fine family project. For Thanksgiving try gluing tiny pieces of cornhusk and dried grass stalks in the typical pyramid shape of corn shocks to small rectangular pieces of cardboard of a color suitable for your whole scheme. At the base of the miniature corn shocks, glue orange fire thorn berries to look like a mound of pumpkins.

Or you might cut a piece of heavy metallic gold, silver, or copper foil in the shape of a tiny compote, paste it on a piece of cardboard, and make a tiny fruit arrangement on it. You could glue on red berries for apples, purple privet berries for grapes, and seeds for nuts, or you could use the artificial miniature fruit made for dollhouses.

However, people are no longer limiting their hospitality to tables at Thanksgiving. More and more you are seeing doors decorated. This is a lovely custom, for it is a way of saying "Welcome" at a joyous season.

Instead of hanging a few ears of Indian corn, however, why not go a step further and make a swag? By using a block of Styrofoam for a base, this is really quite simple. The size block you need depends on how large a design you want, but for one that is about three feet from top to bottom, you would need a piece at least six by four inches and two inches thick. Wrap two pieces of strong wire around the block, one horizontally and one vertically, fastening the ends together in back to form a loop for hanging it on the door.

I find that it is easiest to make the swag in place right on the door. In this way you can keep your design in proportion to the background space as you work. Unless I am using something that has a stiff stem of its own, I wire each piece of material to a florist's pick so that it can be stuck in the Styrofoam block. If this is done securely, the wind or the opening and closing of the door will not disturb the arrangement.

There is a wealth of material to use at this season. What you choose depends on the color of your door, for the swag should be in contrast with this background. Perhaps your door is brown or dark green. Either of these would be a perfect background for a swag made of dried material in the colors ranging from golden beige to dark brown. There are wheat, sea oats, grasses, corn, dried okra, various dried palm, brown dock, brown yucca pods, cattails, and locust pods, to name but a few.

I establish the top, bottom, and outer edges of my design with some of the spiky lighter-colored material, and then work toward the middle, solidifying the outside lines with some of the darker slender material, and work toward the focal point in the center with other interesting forms. You might use wheat or sea oats or reed grass for the outer lines, cattail or dock against them, and fluted yucca pods and boat-shaped milkweed pods toward the center. You can have a ribbon bow in the middle, or one made from natural material—ribbon grass, cornhusks that have been soaked in hot water until they are pliable, bent rattail cones or boiled locust pods. Bend this natural material into loops, wire it into the size bow you wish, fasten it to a florist's pick and stick it into the block at the focal point.

If you have a white door, you could use some of the colorful dried material like orange lantern plant, yellow yarrow, mother-of-pearl honesty, and some green or brown foliage.

You could make a swag that features the symbol of hospitality, the pineapple. In order to anchor the pineapple firmly at the focal point, instead of using the Styrofoam block I use a rectangle of hardware cloth—the heavy wire mesh described in the section on Mechanics. Wires can be put through the center of the pineapple, top and bottom, to wire it firmly to the hardware cloth. If you also wire a small piece of Styrofoam to the back of the hardware cloth, it will make it stand away from the door so that you can insert other material on florist's picks into the hardware cloth. You can use either dried material or greens for the body of the swag, but it is attractive to use fruits or vegetables clustered around the focal pineapple. They might be small artichokes, tiny scrubbed potatoes, pomegranates, or yellow apples.

A unique door decoration uses an Osage orange for the center of a Thanksgiving wreath. Osage oranges are the large yellowish green fruits of the maclura tree which is native in many of our states. This fruit probably got its name because the tree was a favorite of the Osage Indians, who used the wood for making bows. The fruit is inedible but is filled with a milklike fluid which keeps living stems fresh when they are thrust in it. Using the orange as the center, make a solid wreath of green around it by sticking pieces of evergreen material directly into it. Boxwood would be particularly pretty in this instance, as it makes a neat wide wreath. Make a circle of color around the green orange by sticking little sprays of orange fire thorn berries around the inner circle of the wreath. To hang it, put a piece of very heavy wire or a long meat skewer through the wreath from top to bottom. Make a loop at the top, fasten pieces of green and orange velvet ribbon to the loop, and tie the ends into a bow to hang on a nail in the door.

If you don't want a decoration on your door, why not have one at your doorstep? This could be as formal as a garden-type urn filled with chrysanthemums, or as simple as a wooden scrap basket filled with autumn leaves, or a wooden trough filled with pumpkins, colorful squash, gourds, and Indian corn.

Sometimes Thanksgiving arrangements just evolve. This happened to me this year. A friend was given some beautiful tall stalks of love apples—the brown stems thickly clustered with the round yellow-red fruit—and asked me for suggestions how to use it. Since the color scheme of her Early American room is in shades of green with cream and yellow accents, I saw at once that this could be a dramatic color accent. I also thought it should be set off by dark green, and since the stalks were so tall it could be a large arrangement to go on the floor at the entrance from the living room to the dining room. With this in mind we started looking for containers. My first thought was something black—an iron pot or a tall tea caddy—but she didn't have anything like that. Then I discovered a tall gray stone jug. This was fine in size, shape, and texture, but we needed something to tie in the color.

I happened to look out the window and saw just the thing—quantities of waxy gray bayberries. We picked long pieces of bayberry, stripping off the leaves, leaving just the clusters of berries bunched along the stems. We also cut some lovely pine branches. With the pine and bayberry forming the silhouette of the arrangement, and the stalks of red fruit spraying from a group clustered at the focal point, the result was spectacularly satisfying. Mechanics? We filled the jug with sand. The pine branches went in soft-drink bottles of water sunk in the sand. The other material, since it needed no water, was put directly in the sand.

CHRISTMAS

I S THERE anything that is more fun to do at Christmas time, or anything that gives you more Christmas spirit, than to go foraging for greens and other plant material to make your own decorations? Whether you are crunching through the snow in a New England pine forest, cutting blazing poinsettias in Florida, gathering myriads of pine cones in California, or picking luxuriant holly in the Pacific Northwest, there is something about assembling your own decorations that is smugly satisfying.

In the area in which I live there is the combination of seashore and beautiful holly trees, which to me is thrilling. Last year, on a day when the snowy ground and the brilliant blue sky seemed to vie to see which could sparkle the most, I gathered armfuls of holly from tall trees which stood on the bank of a river in view of the open ocean. I loved it!

There are three basic decorations that most of us picture when we think of Christmas—a wreath, a garland or swag, and a Christmas tree. Let's think about ways to make and use them.

Wreaths

A bushy green wreath, tied with a bright red bow is lovely in its own fragrant simplicity. I will never forget a square white Colonial house on a snowy hillside I saw one Christmas Eve. The front of the house was floodlit, and on the outside of every window was a green pine wreath, hung with a large red bow.

It is fun to make a wreath of greens. First you need a circular foundation. You can make this by cutting pliable wands of shrubs like privet or forsythia. Cut pieces of equal length, and bind them tightly together in a circle. Or, you can bend a coat hanger into the proper shape, using the hook to hang the wreath. If you don't want to go to the trouble of making your own, you can buy wire foundation hoops at the florist's. Make a loop of wire at the top so that you can hang it.

Gather evergreens and cut them into four- or five-inch pieces. Then wire the pieces into little bunches, using about five pieces for each bunch. You can use the same kind of greens, or combine several varieties. When you have a number of little bunches prepared, take a spool of heavy wire and wire each one on the hoop, all in the same direction, turning the spool around and around the wreath in a continuous line.

You can also buy foundation hoops of Styrofoam or other plastic substances. In this case you would stick individual pieces of green directly into the hoop, making sure that all sides are thickly covered.

There are many ways that you can decorate a plain green wreath. One way is to make a Della Robbia design, patterned after the enamel-covered terra-cotta fruit and cone wreaths made famous by the artists of the Florentine Della Robbia family. I saw a handsome one recently on the door of a formal Georgian house. The large green pine wreath had a complete inner wreath of brightly colored artificial fruit—bunches of small grapes of different colors, small lemons, walnuts, apples, limes, and cones. It was tied with a big rosette bow of red ribbon lined with green, with streamers. This wreath was a good choice, since the fruit was artificial and the bow of waterproof ribbon and it would look fresh in any weather.

This was a very gay and bright Della Robbia wreath. They are equally lovely in more subdued colors. If your door is protected from the weather, it would be fun to make one in more muted colors with real fruit. Use greens that have more gray in them than the bright green pine. Instead of a whole circle of fruit, you could wire small clusters of real fruit—yellow lady apples, bronze Seckel pears, yellow-red love apples (solanum), and gray-blue juniper berries—to florist's picks and stick the clusters at intervals around the wreath. A moss-green velvet bow would be pretty with this. If you shellac the real fruit it will last longer.

Fruits that are good to use for Della Robbia wreaths are lady apples, crab apples, lemons, limes, kumquats, cranberries, nuts, tangerines, mandarins, Seckel pears, and small pine cones.

Sometimes there is a color problem in decorating the doorway of a house. I am thinking of one that has two lovely antique lanterns with amber glass panels on either side of the doorway. At Christmas a green pine wreath is hung under each lantern, and instead of the usual Christmas red the wreaths are tied with bows of velvet ribbon of the same golden yellow as the amber glass, with a few brown cones dusted with gold clustered around the bows for accent.

You might want to decorate a green wreath to emphasize unusual colors in your living room, as a friend of mine did last year. Her living room has yellow walls, and the other main colors in the room are a rosy rust, the color of Tokay grapes, and a yellow moss-green. She decorated a lovely full pine wreath with bunches of artificial Tokay grapes, and clusters of dried material that particularly delighted her because they were the same unusual green she had used in her room—solid pine cones, sweet gum balls, and acorns. Although these things are usually brown, she had found them at an earlier stage of coloration, and they stayed that way. Hung over the fireplace, the wreath brought all the colors in the room together.

A wreath of gilded nuts against a green wreath is lovely. Clusters of silver-colored bells wired on florist's picks and stuck at intervals around a green wreath, with the bow formed from a string of sleigh bells, gives a musical as well as a fragrant welcome to a visitor.

Another kind of wreath that is fascinating to make is one of pine cones, nuts, and seed pods like the one in Fig. 32. These are perhaps the most fun of all to create. First of all there is the excitement of finding the materials. You can be on the lookout all during the year for things that would be pretty in your Christmas wreath. Also, when your friends know that you like to make this kind of wreath, they will send you surprises. Last Christmas my wreath had coconut calyxes from Florida, wood roses from Hawaii, and cones from California, in addition to the things I found myself.

To make these wreaths you will need a wide circle of Masonite, wallboard, or similar material, a can of linoleum paste—the kind used in laying a linoleum floor—and a wide putty knife to spread

Arrangement by Katherine N. Cutler

Figure 32. A wreath of pods and cones mounted on a Masonite base. (Photo by Roche)

the paste. If you don't want to cut the foundation circle yourself, you can have it done at a lumberyard. Then assemble all your cones, pods, and other things on a newspaper-covered table and go to work.

Fasten a wire loop around the top of the wreath for hanging it. Spread the paste on the background circle generously, as you work in each area. You feel as though you are lavishly icing a cake with frosting of just the right consistency. As in any flower arrangement, plan a design.

You will first need something that will give a finished look to the outer and inner edges. Individual petals cut from large California or Southern cones, pressed into the paste at the edges with the rounded side out, will give a scalloped effect. (If these cones don't grow near you, you can buy them at a florist's. One or two will yield a quantity of petals.) You can use small cones like tiny casuarinas of the same approximate size for the border, or you might use almonds, with the pointed ends out.

When the outer and inner borders are completed, make a focal point or center of interest at the top of the wreath, and another at the bottom. For good balance, the one at the bottom should be larger. Use some of the larger, more interesting shapes for these areas like wood roses, deodora cones (like wooden gardenias), coconut calyxes, or pine cones cut in half. The cut end looks like a flower. Next, make smaller centers of interest in the middle of the sides of the circle. Then, to lead your eye around the circle, between the centers of interest use curved material like curved cones or locust pods. Now you have established a basic design, and you can fill in solidly with the rest of the material.

Use plenty of paste, smearing it on thickly. The nice thing about this substance is that although it eventually gets completely hard, it takes several hours, so, if you want to make some changes in the design after you complete the wreath, you can.

When the wreath is finished, you can either leave it in its natural shades of brown coloring, or you can dust it with silver or gold, or spray it solidly with those colors. It is effective by itself tied with a two-toned green and brown bow, or you can fasten it to a larger green wreath, where it makes a striking inner circle against the dark green. This makes a good "indoor outdoor" wreath. Hung against glass, the green shows from the outside, and the green and gold is attractive from the inside.

Making these wreaths looks like such fun that onlookers want to get into the act. Last year a neighbor doctor, who was having a well-earned Christmas vacation, came in as I was working. He said, "That looks like fun. I'm going to make a 'Beachcomber's Wreath.'" He went for a walk on the beach and gathered his material. He had mussel shells, crab claws, bits of sea glass, bits of cork, a fish lure, clamshells of various sizes, smooth pebbles, some little pieces of curvy wood, cat's-eye shells, and some mallow pods and cones he picked up on the path to the beach. He made the wreath with these things, and the interesting thing is that what started out as a tongue-in-cheek joke turned out to be perfectly beautiful. When the wreath was sprayed heavily with gold, it was a fascinating study in texture, since some of the material was very smooth, and some very rough. His wife hung it on a green wreath for background, and it was a conversation piece for the rest of the holidays.

If you live in a city apartment or a house that is so well-heated that your fireplace is unused, you can use this method to make an attractive decoration to cover the fireplace opening. Cut the Masonite background in the shape of a large fan to stand in front of the opening, and, using linoleum paste, cover it with cones, pods, and other dried material. The center of interest would be at the base, with the other material radiating from it.

Swags and
Garlands

If, instead of a wreath or other decoration on your door, you want a swag, use the same method described for making the Thanksgiving swag, with a base of Styrofoam and the material stuck directly in it. If you are using very heavy branches, you will have to wire them together instead.

A simple but very effective swag for a Christmas door can be made by using large curved branches of white pine. In the center fasten three huge sleigh bells, made by cutting the conventional slotted openings in Styrofoam balls and then spraying the bells gold.

You might want color on the swag. You could use dried flowers or clusters of artificial fruit.

Many houses have a long narrow window on a stair landing. A swag, made in a Hogarth or S curve, is an attractive decoration for the inside of such a window. You can make one very quickly, by finding two long graceful evergreen branches that curve naturally in the right direction, and putting them into Styrofoam, or wiring them together. Make the transition to the focal point in the center with shorter branches, following the same direction, and use some objects like curved cones or pods in the center of interest at the middle to complete the design.

Roping for garlands is easy to make. Do be careful, though, in getting greens from the woods, not to use conservation material like prince's pine, which is becoming all too scarce. Also, while hemlock is nice used in combination with other things, it drops more quickly than some of the other evergreens and therefore is not the best choice for a whole garland. Broad-leafed evergreens, like laurel and rhododendron, are pretty combined with the long-needled ones.

For a foundation use several strands of twine wound together, or heavy cotton rope. Secure the rope at one end so that you can hold it taut as you work. Cut four-inch tips from the evergreen plant material and wire them into little bunches. Then wire

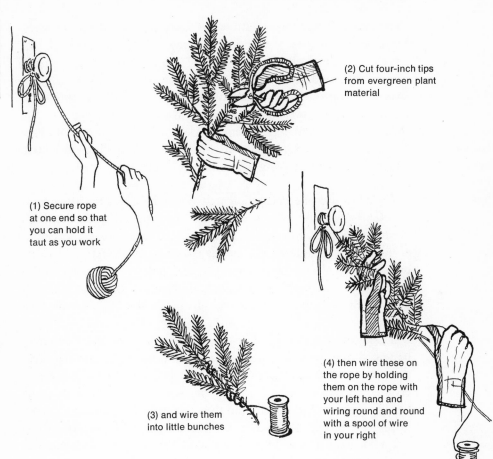

(1) Secure rope at one end so that you can hold it taut as you work

(2) Cut four-inch tips from evergreen plant material

(3) and wire them into little bunches

(4) then wire these on the rope by holding them on the rope with your left hand and wiring round and round with a spool of wire in your right

these on the rope by holding them on the rope with your left hand, and wiring round and round with a spool of wire in your right. Overlap the bunches so that they won't drop down and leave a gap.

For old-fashioned garlands and swags we usually use the so-called Christmas greens like pine, cedar, and spruce—but there are many others that are suitable. Laurel, rhododendron, magnolia, euonymous, and ivy are smooth and green. For color there is variegated ivy, yellow and white variegated holly, yellow varie-gated euonymous, blue-gray Atlantic cedar (Cedrus atlantica), and the browns of glycerin-treated foliage.

Roping is lovely festooned on the stairway, wound on banisters, or draped on fireplaces or over doorways. It can be trimmed like wreaths, in the Della Robbia manner with fruits, or with gilded cones, nuts, real flowers in water picks and gay ribbon.

If you want a shaped or stylized garland for your fireplace, instead of using roping you can cut a garland or swag just the shape and size you want from chicken wire or stiffer hardware cloth. Use this as a foundation, wire greens and other decorative material on it, and hang it on two or more small nails.

Christmas trees

Probably the one decoration that says Christmas to everyone is the Christmas tree. Trimming the Christmas tree is the high point of all pre-Christmas celebration, and it remains the center of festivity throughout the holiday season. Each family has its own traditional way of trimming it, and woe be to the ones who try to make them change. I have even heard it said that this is a major conflict between brides and grooms in the first year of marriage.

There are other ways of using a Christmas tree in addition to having it the main feature. One of my favorites is the flat tree, illustrated in the drawings on page 207. It is easy to make and can be used in many ways. To make the foundation, take a piece of heavy wire or thin metal and bend it into a triangular shape, bringing the ends together in the middle and widening them out again to form a base like a simulated tub. Cover the triangular or tree part with chicken wire, bending the raw edges of the chicken wire around the outline. Fasten a piece of thick branch between the tree and the base to make a trunk.

Take evergreen tips about five inches long and weave them in the chicken wire until you have a solid bushy flat tree. When you make the cuttings, try to select ones with pointed ends, and use these for the outside edges. It is easiest to put in the top point first, and then two symmetrical pieces for the bottom sides. In this way you establish the triangular shape of the tree in the beginning. Cover the base with cardboard, foil, or whatever will go best with your planned decoration.

These trees hang flat, and are good to use against a door, or to put on the wall over a mantel. One Christmas a friend endeared herself to all the neighborhood children with one of these trees. She made dozens of delicious little popcorn balls and wrapped

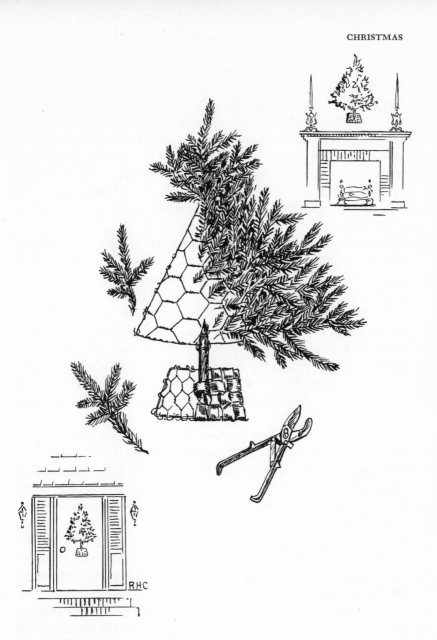

them in red cellophane paper. She hung one of the trees on her front door and decorated it with the popcorn balls, stuck into the tree with florist's picks. The finishing touch was a big red bow tied around the trunk of the tree, from which hung streamers of red ribbons and little bells. It was soon noised around the neighborhood that the children were welcome to help themselves to the popcorn balls. When my friend heard the bells tinkling, she knew the time had come to replace the balls on the tree with fresh ones she kept ready in a bowl in the hallway.

Another charming way to decorate one of these trees for an outside door is to put a bunch of holly, loaded with berries, in the center and fasten two artificial red birds on the tree, as though, attracted by the holly berries, they had paused in flight.

I like to put one of these trees over my mantel and trim it with real flowers. Sometimes I am fortunate enough to get paper-white narcissus blooms. These, put in water picks, look like clusters of white Christmas stars, and their fragrance, mingled with that of the tree, is enchanting. At other times I use white freesias, which last a long time as the buds continue to open. I have also used pink or red carnations.

A wrought-iron spray to hold flowerpots makes the basis for an attractive Christmas tree door decoration. You can make cones of chicken wire so that the base of the cone fits in the pots. Stick pieces of pine through the chicken wire to form little trees. Insert a tree in each pot and tie a red ribbon around it, ending in a bow. You will have a graceful spray of perky little trees adorning your door.

Sometimes the simplest decorations are the most effective. We visited a house one Christmas where this was true. The family had moved in just before the holidays, and the house needed to be completely redecorated inside. Instead of fretting that things weren't just the way she wanted them as a background for her usual distinctive decorations, the mother engineered a "greens gathering day." The whole family, equipped with thermos bottles of hot soup and a hamper of hearty sandwiches, went tramping through the New England woods and fields collecting many little evergreen trees about two feet high. Back home they put the trees in white pots, tied a big saucy red bow on them, and put them all around the house—on tables, the hearth, on the stair landing, on mantelpieces and wide window sills. When you walked in that house and were greeted by the fragrance of the greens and the perky little trees with their festive bows, you didn't notice the dingy wallpaper—you just thought, "Christmas is here."

For modern houses, there is a stylized Christmas tree that is attractive to make. You use the same triangular shape as for the flat green ones, but instead of wire and chicken wire you make the frame from Masonite or wallboard. In the same way that you make the cone and pod wreaths, and using the same materials, you make a solid tree to hang on the wall or over the fireplace. For rooms in the neutral tones often used in these houses, you will probably leave the cones and dried material in their natural coloring, although just dusting it lightly with a gold spray will add Christmas sparkle. A very tall slender stylized tree can be made in this same way, and is pretty to use in these houses as a wall panel. It can be floor to ceiling height, if you wish. An appropriate ornament for a mantel or coffee table in a house of this type is one of the little nut and cone trees described in the chapter on Thanksgiving tables.

Before we leave the subject of Christmas trees let's not forget the birds. It is such fun to make decorations and trim an outdoor tree just for them. At the top have a white star, made by covering a wire frame thickly with peanut butter and sticking popcorn in it. You can make icicles of popcorn, stuck together with peanut butter. Make baskets from hollowed-out grapefruit and orange rinds, and fill them with bacon fat. Make balls of suet, raisins, and seeds, and wreaths of cranberries. Your decorations may not last long, but you'll have wonderful fun watching the birds enjoy them.

Probably next in importance to Christmas trees come Christmas tables. A beautifully decorated and appointed table sets the scene for festive dining. And it isn't only dinner tables that are important.

Tables

I remember one Christmas in a house full of young children where the day started very early. On the table in the breakfast room was an arrangement that did as much to open our sleepy eyes as the smell of the hot coffee from the kitchen. On a piece of white marble was an arrangement of green, red, and white fruits and vegetables, whose line of design started in the curving tail feathers of a white ceramic rooster with a bright red comb. This rooster was placed high on the fruit at the left of the arrangement, and the design line followed through a grouping of red apples, green pears, broccoli, little white onions, green grapes, and pebbly dark green spinach leaves, and ended in the upswept tail feathers of another rooster placed on the table at the right.

I have a friend who always uses a fruit arrangement for her

Christmas dinner centerpiece. As a container she uses a family heirloom that has been used at the holiday season in her family for almost a hundred years—a white and gold luster compote. She uses a pineapple for height, and tries to find one that is more green than brown with a top whose leaves have a decided curve. She emphasizes this by pulling out a few (the same idea as shaping eyebrows). She sprays the brown part gold, leaving it unpainted where it is green, and leaves the top green also. All the rest of the fruits, except limes and avocados, which she leaves their natural green color, she also sprays gold. She uses a tangerine or two, and some kumquats, because the texture of the skin looks grainy when painted, and makes an interesting contrast to the satin smooth appearance of grapes, pears, and apples. The gold fruit, with the natural green limes and avocados, with some fresh laurel leaves, on a soft green damask cloth has great distinction and elegance used with china with a wide gold border. The sprayed fruit lasts at least two weeks. This is an idea for someone who cannot use red in a dining room.

For another table, you might use a white damask cloth and china with touches of red and green in the border. You could have a long low centerpiece (perhaps arranged in one of the glass bowls that fit in a low candlestick) with white snapdragons tapering to green buds at the tips, extending horizontally, sprays of ivy following the line of the snapdragons, and thickly berried holly and a few red carnations toward the center.

For a less formal table in an Early American house, in a dining room furnished with old pieces of pine, a copper scoop filled with red and green fruit, apples, red and green peppers, and green grapes, with pieces of holly used as foliage would be appropriate. You could put some of the fruit on the table at the back of the arrangement, where the back of the scoop curves up.

Perhaps your dining room is one in which yellow looks best as the featured color. You can still have a very Christmasy table by using a gray-green cloth, a silver bowl filled with yellow roses, yellow-bordered variegated holly, gold-tipped green cedar, and green grapes. The finishing touch would be gray-green bayberry candles in silver candlesticks.

There is a pretty table decoration that children love to make at Christmas. Gather dried weeds and grasses from the fields and roadside—dock, milkweed pods, dried Queen Anne's lace, in fact anything that is stiff and an interesting shape—bring them home, put them on sheets of newspaper, and spray them with silver paint. When they are dry, you can arrange them by sticking the stiff stems in a ball of florist's clay. A little glitter sprinkled on some of the material while it is wet adds a sparkly touch. You can paint the clay foundation silver also. This arrangement is lovely placed on a mirror.

The Christmas dinner table that I remember as most typifying Christmas to me was in a gracious New England dining room. There were eighteen people seated at the table, including a year-old baby and a ninety-year-old grandfather. A fire was burning in the fireplace, and huge snowflakes were falling outside the bowed window. The table decoration was smartly sophisticated in design for adult tastes, and amusing in subject for the children. The long table was covered by a white cloth. A very wide red satin ribbon, with a green one not quite as wide on top of it, ran down the middle of the table, hanging down to the edge of the cloth on each end. In the center was a handsome red and gold sleigh filled with holly, sprigs of green, and tiny gaily wrapped packages. It was driven by a jolly Santa Claus, brandishing a whip over six pairs of white reindeer with red and gold harnesses.

Kitchen   Don't forget the kitchen at Christmas. Little Della Robbia wreaths for the windows would be charming, made on a Styrofoam base with laurel leaves. If the Styrofoam wreath is too thick, slice it in half with a sharp knife. Wash the laurel leaves well, and rub them to a gloss with waxed paper. Then pin individual overlapping leaves on the circle until it is covered. Wire small artificial fruits into a circle, and fasten it against the laurel by sticking small brads or hairpins into the Styrofoam through the leaves at intervals.

You can make a Della Robbia tree for the wall, instead, if you'd rather. You might use a salt box fastened to the wall as a base to hold a triangular "tree" of wallboard. Glue laurel leaves around the edge for a border, and fill the center solidly with fruit.

My favorite kitchen decoration is a green wreath of fresh herbs. This stays fresh quite a long time, especially if you sprinkle it with a little water and put it in a cool place overnight. The nice part, though, is that you can let it dry in place and enjoy its spicy fragrance after Christmas is over (as well as snitching a few leaves to put in the soup or stew).

Candles   Christmas also makes us think of candles. The warmth of their soft glow adds to the general spirit of this holiday season. There are many ways to use them, besides the obvious ones.

An antique candle mold, backed by branches of evergreen, sweeping high on one side, and low on the other, filled with red candles graduated in size to follow the curve of the branches, would be a cheery greeting on a hall table. Always be sure, though, when you combine greens and candles, that the greens won't come in contact with the candles as they burn.

The round Oasis holders that are mentioned in Mechanics make ideal containers for candle and flower and greens arrangements. A large round candle three inches in diameter will fit in the inner circle, where the round plug of Oasis usually goes. Fasten the candle securely with florist's clay or Stickum. You can pack the outer circle with wet Oasis and make an arrangement around the base of the candle. An attractive one would be the traditional holly and ivy, or you could use sprigs of evergreen with red garnet roses or small red carnations. You could use this candle arrangement flat on the table, or make it very important by putting it on a small silver, pewter, or colored-glass compote. (A plain glass compote wouldn't have enough visual weight for the heavy candle.)

Three large round red candles of different heights, on a wooden lazy Susan, their base surrounded by greens, would be a stunning and easy-to-fix arrangement for a round pine coffee table. In a more formal house, you could put a large green candle in the middle of a gold pine and pod wreath on a coffee table.

If you don't want to use a bright color, white poinsettias combined with greens at the base of a white candle make a pleasing arrangement. Be careful, though, in selecting the color of your candle, for poinsettias are not a dead white, and you will need to match it with a candle in one of the off-white shades.

Kissing Balls   No house would be completely decorated for Christmas without a "kissing ball." These hold a sprig of mistletoe and are hung in an inside doorframe or under a chandelier. There are many legends surrounding the kissing ball, some of them dating from the ancient pagans. No two are alike, but it is agreed that anyone who stands under the mistletoe on a kissing ball may be kissed.

One way to make these delightful ornaments is to use the two circles of an embroidery hoop. Cover the hoops by winding them with ribbon. You can wind one with green ribbon and one with red, or you might use a two-toned gold and red ribbon for both. A very dressy way to decorate a hoop is to sew pearls at intervals to red velvet ribbon, and then glue the ribbon to the outside of the hoop and green velvet ribbon to the inside.

When the hoops are covered, fit one inside the other so that they make a round cage to hold a sprig of mistletoe fastened to the top, where the circles cross, with a ribbon bow.

Another way to make a different kissing ball is to run a long meat skewer through a big apple. Cover the apple completely, making a round green ball, by sticking pieces of a shiny evergreen like boxwood, ilex, or azalea into the apple. (The moisture in the apple will keep it fresh.) Decorate the ball by scattering tiny red bows over it, sticking them into the apple with pearl-topped corsage pins. Fasten a cluster of mistletoe to the bottom of the ball by wiring it onto the exposed end of the skewer, making sure that the latter is covered. Wind the top end of the skewer with narrow red ribbon, and hang it by a ribbon bow in the round eye.

Crèches

A crèche, or nativity scene, is another thing that is always associated with Christmas. This is, of course, symbolic of the beginning of Christmas, depicting as it does the birth of Christ. In many households the figures of the scene are treasured from year to year. They are brought out on the first Sunday in Advent and assembled. In other families a crèche is put under the tree on Christmas Eve.

Last year I wanted to make one of these scenes in a small wall niche. I found some charming nativity figures carved from light wood. They are rather stark and simple, and I wanted to keep the whole scene that way—a contrast to the lush, brightly colored ones we sometimes see. I lined the back and sides of the niche with midnight blue paper. In the corners I grouped live miniature date palms, which I had taken temporarily out of their pots and put in water in cup needlepoint holders. I hid the holders with flat rocks and covered the bottom of the niche with sand. When the figures were in place I hung a silver star on a practically invisible thread from the top of the niche and lighted the scene with a tiny bulb concealed in the top of the molding. There really was a look of desert mystery to the little scene.

In the background of a nativity scene you might want to use pointed sprays of dark green juniper to simulate cypress trees, and pieces of furry gray-green cedar for olive trees. You could use sand or dirt on the floor, and put tiny tips of pine here and there to look like scrub growth. A few flat rocks would also make it look natural.

A flat shallow basket, hung on the wall like a shadow box, makes a good background for a nativity scene. You can leave the basket in its natural color or paint it according to your general decorative scheme. It can contain the complete scene or perhaps just a lovely figure of the Madonna, surrounded by greens.

NEW YEAR'S EVE AND DAY

B Y NEW YEAR'S EVE people are beginning to tire a little of Christmas decorations, so it is a good time to store them and put fresh flowers around the house. You can make a New Year's Eve table very gay. Instead of flowers on the buffet table, you can feature other things with greens. Against a green background you can make an arrangement of bright-colored balloons of different shapes, or colored streamers in fantastic curves, or noisemakers and the "snappers" that children love at birthday parties, covered with bright-colored crepe paper, grouped artistically.

New Year's Day is a traditional one for open house. For this the table would be similar to a tea table, except that instead of a tea service at one end and a coffee service at the other, you would probably substitute a punch bowl of eggnog or milk punch for one or the other. You could have a punch bowl, instead, featured on a smaller table, and instead of a centerpiece, wreath the bottom of the bowl with a flat garland of green leaves, and place camellias or gardenias around it at intervals.

VALENTINE'S DAY

V ALENTINE'S DAY is a sentimental holiday. It brings to mind young lovers, red hearts, dainty lace, cupids, and old-fashioned flowers like bleeding hearts, pansies, forget-me-nots, rose-buds, mignonettes, and garden pinks. Old-fashioned containers like

Arrangement by Abigail Spies

Figure 33. This arrangement, titled "A Valentine for Mother," was made by an eight-year-old junior garden club member. It is a good example of the excellent work of which children are ca-pable. Snapdragons, daisies, and anemones follow an S-curve de-sign, which is repeated in the cupid forming the base of the container. (Photo by Roche)

epergnes, compotes, cupids holding bowls like the one in Fig. 33, and Victorian fan-shaped vases are suitable for these flowers.

Cloths for Valentine tables are of lace, or fine linens in pastel shades.

If you aren't the pastel type, you can have a striking table by using a red cloth. Cut various-sized hearts out of very heavy red paper and fasten a wire to each. Cover the wire with green floral tape. Now you have heart "flowers" and can make an arrangement of them for the center of the table, using green foliage like euonymous, laurel, huckleberry, or lemon leaf. Or you could make Valentine topiary trees by fastening an apple on a slim green wooden rod and sticking the rod in a lump of floral clay. Make a round "tree" in the apple by sticking snips of green like ilex, boxwood, or pine in it. Scatter little red paper hearts over it, fastening each with a tiny piece of Stickum.

If someone sends you long-stemmed red roses for a Valentine, be brave and cut those beautiful long stems into different lengths. I know it is hard to do, but the finished arrangement will be so much prettier than if it is topheavy with the roses all at the same level.

EASTER

ALTHOUGH Easter is essentially a religious festival day, it has also come to mean a holiday that is important to children, and one that adults enjoy because it heralds spring.

There are suitable decorations for Easter tables, suggested by all of these things. Symbolic of the religious connotation is the Easter lily, and few tables are lovelier than one set with a handsome white cloth, gold banded china, and a centerpiece of Easter lilies with their buds.

Children look forward to coloring Easter eggs, having jelly bean hunts and presents of Easter baskets of candy and toy rabbits and chickens. When children are dyeing eggs, have them do some for the Easter table centerpiece. On a table using a cream or yellow cloth, you could have a centerpiece of forsythia branches, with yellow, lavender, brown, and orange eggs nestled at the base. For a different color scheme, you might use a pink cloth with forced quince blossoms, and pink, rose, blue, and lavender eggs.

The children can also make place cards for the table. Break off the tip of a raw egg, empty it, and when it is dry paint it a color to match the centerpiece. Make stands for the eggs by folding a piece of heavy paper and cutting a tiny semicircle at the fold for the egg to rest in. Fill the egg with a little nosegay, and put one at each place. Or you can fill the egg with dirt and plant a tiny plant in it, later putting it in the garden, eggshell and all.

Children can make other pretty Easter favors by painting empty spools a pretty color. Paste a piece of foil on the bottom of each and stuff the little hole with crumbled wet Oasis. Use grape hyacinths, violets, or sprigs of fruit blossoms stuck in the Oasis to simulate a little plant.

A very simple table arrangement, but one that could only mean Easter, would be to use a pretty round hatbox for a container. Put something inside to hold water, and fill it with flowers that are typically spring, and typically Easter colors—forsythia, daffodils, pussy willows, violets, and purple pansies.

If you want to be different, and have a fruit arrangement instead of flowers, use yellow Norway maple branches, eggplants, lemons, yellow pears, and purple grapes.

If a pastel or a yellow and purple Easter table doesn't suit your house, try making a naturalistic arrangement on a brown or green cloth, using gnarled bare branches, with moss and small spring flowers like crocuses, violets, or scillas at the bottom. Put chocolate rabbits in various poses on the moss as though they were playing there.

HALLOWE'EN

HALLOWE'EN means jack-o'-lanterns, trick-or-treating, and the combination of orange and black colors.

It isn't only children who like to make jack-o'-lanterns. Teen-agers and grown-ups too like to carve pumpkins into grinning or grotesque faces, sometimes with appendages like green pepper ears and carrot noses. Usually these are placed at the front door, but there are other places where they look equally at home. Try putting one on your lantern or fence post. Or make a nice big cheerful one and put it lighted in a prominent window in a darkened room.

For a buffet table centerpiece, it would be attractive to fasten small jack-o'-lanterns to the candle cups of a black wrought-iron candelabrum, and have lighted candles inside. Or it would be striking to combine orange flowers like calendulas, marigolds, or cockscombs with orange-veined croton leaves in a black container.

Some children I know have a charming custom at Hallowe'en. They hollow out tiny pumpkins and fill them with chrysanthemums, wild asters, or goldenrod and leave them as gifts at the houses where they go "trick-or-treating."

If you are having a Hallowe'en party it is amusing to make your flower arrangements in seasonal colors like the one in Fig. 34.

Arrangement by Myra Brooks

Figure 34. Fall garden flowers in shades of yellow and orange are arranged in an Oriental container on a black base. Black viburnum berries pick up the color of the base for dramatic accent. (Photo by Roche)

PATRIOTIC

RED, WHITE, and blue is the logical and obvious color scheme for parties on Washington's Birthday, Lincoln's Birthday, Memorial Day, and the Fourth of July. There is a trick to using them, though. Using them in equal parts is weak and ineffective. It is much more dramatic to feature one of the colors with white, and use the other color for an accent.

For instance, you could have a red and white checked cloth, white plates, dark blue tumblers, and white pots of red geraniums. Or you might have a dark blue cloth, white milk glass plates and tumblers, and a milk glass compote of bachelor's buttons and white feverfew with a few red carnations.

It is fun to set a table in red, white, and blue, because if you don't happen to own linen, china, and glassware in these colors, there are many things to buy that are very inexpensive. You can get red, blue, red and white striped, blue and white striped, red and white checked, and blue and white checked fabrics to make cloths. These are especially gay when they are bordered with wide white fringe. You can find at very reasonable prices, plates, tumblers, goblets, and flower containers in deep red, and dark blue glass, and reproduction milk glass.

If you don't want to use a conventional container for flowers, you can make symbolic ones—drums, by painting coffee cans white, and stringing them with red and blue cord, gluing more of the cord around the edges. You can make firecrackers by covering fruit juice cans with red Chinese paper. It would even be fun on Lincoln's Birthday to make a little scene for the center of the table, with pieces of pine for trees, a log cabin made with children's building logs, and a little garden (made from pieces of red geranium, individual florets of feverfew, and pieces of bachelor's button stuck in wet Oasis) around a flagpole flying a flag.

Red, white, and blue flowers are:

Red	White	Blue
Anthurium	Carnation	Anemone
Anemone	Daisy	Bachelor's Button
Camellia	Freesia	Delphinium
Carnation	Feverfew	Grape Hyacinth
Cockscomb	Gladiolus	Iris
Geranium	Stock	Statice
Gladiolus	Sweet Pea	
Rose	Tulip	
Tulip		

V

Using Your Talents for Others

COMMUNITY ACTIVITIES

THE OTHER day I found an old diary of my mother's and was intrigued by an entry she wrote when I was just a little over a year old. It said: "Katherine loves flowers. Whenever she sees one growing, or in a bouquet, she touches it and says 'Oh,' in an awestruck voice." I do believe that many people are born with a love for flowers, and learning to arrange them in a way that adds beauty to their surroundings can bring so much peace and joy. That is why it distresses me when I hear people say they are "afraid" to make an arrangement, or worse, see them trying so hard to conform to some supposed standard that they are nervous wrecks. It should have just the opposite effect. For a person who has learned to cope with mechanics, flower arranging can be tranquilizing and self-absorbing.

However, it is not a selfish art. Believe it or not, a flower arranger can be of great value to her community, her church, and her fellow man. I love the cartoons about flighty portly ladies and their "tra-la-la" approach to flower arranging—in fact I collect them. But most of the flower arrangers I know don't fit the picture. They work too hard to be portly, and their approach is common sense, and often dollars and cents.

How many times has a flower arranger heard a voice at the other end of the telephone say, "Will you do the flowers for the church supper (or the PTA tea, or the Community Chest dinner, or the Scout father and son banquet)?" The voice invariably adds, "Of course we don't have much money to spend."

There you have the problem. As anyone knows who has ever done it, it takes a lot of material to make arrangements for several long tables, including a speakers' table, and unfortunately flowers can be expensive. Also, to be effective, the containers should be similar. If the request comes when there is outdoor material, it isn't as difficult. Some members of the committee may have garden flowers, and there are vines, berries, and wildflowers in woods and along the roadside. The problem of containers is still there, however.

At one church supper the problem was solved in this way. There were plenty of marigolds available—yellow, orange, and the small brown and yellow ones. The small amount of money alloted went to buy two dozen tin bread pans (a permanent investment). These were painted brown. Instead of Oasis, which would have been easy but too expensive, the pans were filled with crumpled chicken wire to hold the flowers. When the arrangements, in shades of yellow, orange, and brown were in place, four together in the center of each long table, with the others spaced toward the ends, the effect was very festive. After the supper the pans were stored away, to be brought out again for a Christmas tea—sprayed gold and filled with greens and green and gold Christmas tree ornaments.

In the autumn, among the prettiest, most appropriate and inexpensive decorations for long tables or many small ones are small pumpkins hollowed out and filled with autumn leaves.

I bless the day that I discovered candle boards—nothing more than pieces of board with holes drilled in them to hold candles. These can be made to hold as many candles as you wish. For a long table, ones holding five are satisfactory. These can be stained, or painted any color. You can either use the same-size candles, or have them graduated from a tall one in the middle. Placed at intervals along the table, with greens or autumn leaves between and around them, they are very effective.

The small Oasis holders, which we have mentioned many times, are a wonderful investment for any place that is apt to have large luncheons or dinners. They are inexpensive, the metal holders last indefinitely, and the little plugs last for several occasions and are replaceable at very little cost. Several can be put together for a long arrangement, or they are ideal to use for small tables. Best of all, there is no problem of mechanics, and once a flower ar-

ranger in charge has made a sample arrangement, other committee members can easily copy them. If there are no flowers, you
can make very attractive arrangements with greens that are readily
available, such as privet or arborvitae.

It is amazing how, with a little thought, you can solve this
problem of "no money." A group of citizens in a seashore town
gave a dinner to honor a well-loved town official who was retiring.
Less money spent on table decorations meant more money for a
gift, so the committee was asked to "dream up something inexpensive." For table decorations for a dinner of three hundred, the
decorations cost exactly nothing.

Everyone at the shore collects driftwood, so the committee
combed the town and borrowed particularly pretty silvery gray
pieces. These they spaced down the middle of the long tables.
On the driftwood, they arranged flat heads of red, white, and pink
mallows, the lovely hibiscuslike flower that grows wild at the seashore. Since the club where the dinner was held was able to supply pale pink cloths for the tables, the whole effect was really
charming.

Another time, a mother was faced with the problem of doing
a table arrangement for a tea the Athletic Association of her
daughter's school was giving for a visiting hockey team. The table
was very long. There was only a couple of dollars in the budget
for flowers, and it was late fall, when a frost had taken the last
of the garden flowers.

She came up with an ingenious solution. She bought eleven
candles of graduated size and a few stalks of spray chrysanthemums.
She fastened the candles, with the tallest in the middle, to a long
narrow board with florist's clay, and put it in the center of the
table. Then she put a hockey stick flat on the table at each end of
the candle board, with the rounded end of the stick next to it. In
the curve of each stick she put a square of well-soaked Oasis. This
held a line arrangement of the chrysanthemum sprays which followed the curve of the hockey stick. She used some of the larger
blossoms broken off and placed at the bottom, with huckleberry
foliage that came with the flowers, for the focal point and to hide
the Oasis. She also stuck little pieces of huckleberry in the clay
at the bottom of the candles to soften the line and hide the clay.

Doing table decorations is not the only way for a flower arranger
to be helpful in the community. There are many places where a

Arranged by members of the Garden Club of Bermuda

Figure 35. Plant material is arranged in a niche to represent an underwater seascape. (Photo by Simons Studio)

lovely arrangement brings pleasure to many people—the library, a hospital, a museum, or the foyer of a YMCA building.

A bright arrangement on a librarian's desk gives the same air of warmth and graciousness to the room that it does in your own house, and think how many people can enjoy it during the day.

A beautiful arrangement in the lobby of a hospital can do much for the morale of the often troubled and apprehensive people who see it. This was proved by the unsolicited and anonymous letter received recently by a garden club. The woman who wrote it was thanking the club for an arrangement done by one of the members that she had seen on her arrival at the hospital for a very serious operation. It was a particularly lovely spring arrangement of pussy willows and daffodils, done in an unusual way. The writer of the letter said that she had been very despondent but that the beautiful arrangement, with its message of beginning life, gave her hope for the first time. She ended by saying that, to her, one such arrangement was worth more than many flower shows.

There are groups of women organized to provide bedside flowers for patients in Veterans Hospitals. On certain days of the week people bring garden flowers to a central point. The women transport them to the hospitals and arrange bedside bouquets. At Christmas and Easter they also trim the chapels and dining rooms.

In a town which has a fine museum, committees of women have done study and research to provide arrangements for certain strategic spots in the museum. These arrangements are authentic and not only contribute to the beauty of the museum but are another aspect of its instruction.

In still another town the money-making project for the Women's Fellowship of a church is to sponsor an antique show in the church hall. Dealers pay for space and give a commission on sales. Some of the women who are interested in flower arrangement make arrangements for all the booths. The dealers feel that this so helps their sales that there is a long waiting list for space at this particular show. Sometimes flower arrangers are called upon to do more elaborate decorative schemes. The one in Fig. 35 could well be used to enhance a museum exhibit of South Seas culture.

These are but a few of the ways a flower arranger can contribute her talent to the community. There is almost no facet of community life where flower arranging hasn't a place.

CHURCH

ARRANGING flowers for services in a church is both challenging and extremely rewarding. It is challenging because there are special problems involved in color, scale, and choice of container, and rewarding because it is a privilege to be able to contribute to a service for the worship and glorification of God. To beautify His house with harmonious arrangements, done in a spirit of reverence and humility, brings great personal spiritual satisfaction, and, like music, creates a setting to lift the spirits of the entire congregation.

I remember one Easter morning when I went early to the church to check the arrangements I had done the day before. The organist and soloist were rehearsing for the morning service. I stood alone in the sanctuary, surrounded by the sweet smell of the lilies, with warm spring sunlight streaming across the altar, listening to the glorious strains of "I Know That My Redeemer Liveth." The message of Easter was never more clear.

Too often the committee in charge of church flowers fulfills its obligation by soliciting money or using that donated as memorials and giving a standing order to a florist. There may not be much money, and he, poor man, is put to it to deliver a sizable bouquet. Consequently it is too frequently a monotonous combination of snapdragons and gladiolus with lots of lemon leaves or huckleberry, delivered in a papier-mâché container or a conventional white pottery urn. Doesn't this seem a pity when, with a small investment in containers and a large investment in awareness of available outdoor plant material, the altar flowers could add so much to the inspiration of the services?

In every congregation there are people who enjoy working with flowers. It is worth while to ferret out these people and organize them into a committee. Arranging church flowers should never be the responsibility of just one person, no matter how talented. There are always times like trips, illnesses, and emergencies when that one person couldn't be available. One or two of the most experienced could give some instruction to the rest of the committee on church arrangements, and it would be interesting for the whole group to study a little about the history of the use of flowers in churches, their association with church ritual, and the symbolism of liturgical color. In this way there would always be willing and able hands to take on the pleasant duty of the flower arrangements.

This committee, too, should be vocal at the time the annual church budget is drawn up and see that some portion of church funds is allotted to flowers. It need not be a great deal. Containers can be inexpensive, and there are donations for memorial flowers. A great part of the year there are outdoor flowers to use. But there are expenses for containers and mechanics, and flowers to be purchased when no others are available, and there should be a fund for this purpose.

In thinking of flower arrangements for a church, the first thing to consider is the architecture of the church building. Is it Gothic, with tall pointed arches? Is it large and massive, with stone walls and vaulted ceilings? Is it a classic Colonial type? This will govern the type of arrangement. It is easy to see that though a mass arrangement would be equally appropriate in either a massive stone church or a classic Colonial one, the first would be larger and more flamboyant, while the second would be simpler and more restrained.

Then there are other things to be considered. Does the church have a chancel, or is the pulpit on a platform behind the Communion table? This would affect the placement. Are the windows stained or clear glass? Is there a dorsal hanging behind the altar or Communion table? This would affect the color. Is the cross on the altar, or does it hang above it? This would affect the size. If the cross is hanging above the altar, it doesn't restrict the size of the arrangement. However, though I have never been able to find a definite prohibitive rule, it is a generally accepted custom that flowers should not dominate the altar cross. An arrangement shouldn't be so tall that it is higher than the cross, or so abundant that it partially hides it. If the cross is small, it can be raised on blocks to allow for a larger arrangement.

A church with stained-glass windows is darker than one with clear glass. Therefore, bright flowers help lighten the interior. For a church with clear glass windows, the colors can be more muted. Also, the predominant color in stained-glass windows may suggest color combinations for arrangements.

A dorsal can be an effective background for altar arrangements, but if it is not taken into consideration, you may end up with a jarring color note that is disconcerting rather than pleasing to the congregation. For instance, if the hanging is a blue-red, there are combinations of lavender and pink that are exquisite against it— but think how awful vases of orange calendulas would be.

The next thing to consider is the type of container. Many churches have handsome altar vases of brass or other metals, but as they are more often than not the type with a narrow hard-to-arrange neck, the flower committee bypasses them instead of conquering them. If you are confronted with such a vase, use it! Choose flowers with slender stems, and do the arrangement by holding it in your hand. Then wire the stems together and stick the whole thing into the neck of the vase at once. If you need a few flowers higher in the arrangement, put them in a long pill bottle, tape the bottle to a heavy wire which you can force into the neck, or even, in extreme cases, fasten to the back of the vase with Stickum. The flowers in front will conceal the bottle. Sometimes tall arrangements on a pedestal, like the ones of calla lilies in Fig. 36, are appropriate for a church. The Portuguese wedges described in the chapter on Mechanics could be useful here to build up the height.

If a church doesn't have handsome vases, the Flower Committee, using some of the money budgeted to them, can buy suitable ones as a permanent investment. There are many inexpensive ceramic vases of good design or classic shape that make excellent church vases. Pottery vases can be painted a color that blends with the other church appointments, or a neutral soft green, gray, or beige. They can be repainted for variation.

I have a tall footed bowl and an urn that are inexpensive replicas of ones in a museum. They are of dull mahogany-colored pottery

Arranged by members of the Garden Club of Bermuda

Figure 36. A typical Bermuda bridal table that would be equally lovely anywhere. Pedestal arrangements of white calla lilies flank the table. The centerpiece is of white snapdragons, roses, sweet peas, orange blossoms, and freesia. The garlands are caught with white passionflowers. An arrangement of fresh roses in a shadow-box frame is over the mantel. (Photo by Simons Studio)

and would be very suitable for a church. I once saw a stunning pair of altar vases made from the tops of wooden newel posts. Even papier-mâché looks elegant when it is painted with a good flat paint.

Flowers for churches should be those with fairly bold forms and good lasting qualities. Dainty flowers are beautiful at close range, but their effectiveness is lost at a distance. There is often outdoor material available to use for arrangements. Members are always happy to contribute from their gardens. A pair of arrangements using garden flowers, like the one in Fig. 36 could be used on either side of the cross. And then there are wildflowers.

I was shocked once to hear a minister object to black-eyed Susans being used on the altar of his beautiful but simple small church. He said they "weren't nice enough." I mentally shouted "Bravo" when I heard the woman who was fixing them say, her black eyes snapping, "God made these flowers just as He made roses and lilies, and I think He loves them just as much!"

If there aren't any flowers available, think about trees. Blazing red and yellow autumn leaves would be stunning in a white Colonial interior, and pine branches lend dignity whenever you use them.

A minister in one church where I worked on the Flower Committee discouraged our using outdoor material because he wanted the altar flowers to be taken to sick people in the parish after the services, and he wanted them "hothouse." It was hard work but we finally convinced him that after flower stems are cut different lengths for a design in one container, they aren't satisfactory to be regrouped into other bouquets, and we set up a separate fund for flowers for the sick and shut-ins, even though sometimes it meant taking only a single rose. However, as I have said before, to me a single perfect rose is lovelier than many bouquets.

It is always best to arrange flowers in church the day before the services, as many churches have early services and you don't want to be rushed. As a precaution, though, one member of the committee should go early on Sunday morning to check and see that nothing is wilted.

When you are working at the altar, always have a large drop cloth at hand so that drops of water won't stain the wood, or bits of plant material be ground in the carpet.

The flowers should look equally well to those who sit in the front pews and those who sit in the back. This presents a problem, as the farther back in the church you are the smaller the arrangement looks. If you make an arrangement on the altar and then back down the aisle, you can almost see it diminish in size before your eyes. For this reason you make the arrangement larger than seems necessary when you are right in front of it. You will find yourself running up and down the center aisle several times to see the effect of height, width, and focal point from the back of the church.

It is important to remember that certain colors like blue and lavender recede with distance. A focal point of blue irises, for example, which may look charming as you are arranging it at the altar, will look like a big hole from a distance. It is safer to avoid these colors, but if you do use them, put foliage in back of the flowers so that they will be silhouetted against it.

There is no set rule for placement of arrangements. It is customary on an altar that is centered by a cross with candlesticks at either end to place the flowers on either side of the cross. The arrangements should be large enough not to look apologetic, and small enough not to be the dominant feature. In a church where the lectern is on a platform in the front of the church, arrangements can be on the floor on either side of the platform, or on a table on it. If the Communion table is on the floor in front of the lectern, an arrangement can be put on it on the Sundays it is not being used for the service.

It is a nice touch to have flowers in the narthex or vestibule of a church. They welcome people as they enter and are pleasant to see as the congregation is filing out.

At Easter and Christmas it is the custom in many churches to decorate with plants, lilies, or poinsettias, so that they can be taken to invalids and shut-ins after the service. If this is so in your church, try to get plants of matching sizes, graduating from large to small. Then you can mass them for a lovely effect. Nothing looks more spotty than individual pots set here and there. Be sure that the pots are covered not with foil, which attracts the light and detracts from the plants, but with pieces of foliage put in front of them.

These plants are prettiest when they are tilted so that you look directly into the flowers. In one church, boxes, like window boxes, except that the back was much lower than the front, were made to fit the railings and stained the color of the wood in the church. Pots in these could be tilted against the front, and wedged against the back, so that the flowers in them seemed to be growing naturally in the boxes. You can also borrow stands from a florist which permit pots to be tilted forward.

Sometimes people wish to give memorial flowers on a particular Sunday. I am sure that the donor would rather give the money to the committee and let it buy and arrange the flowers, if the committee lets it be known that it is willing to do so, rather than give an impersonal order to a florist.

Sometimes, too, there are occasions when you have no choice and must use given flowers. I am thinking of the time the sister of a member of the congregation sent several dozen pink anthuriums to her from Hawaii to be used at the Sunday services as a memorial to their mother. We used them in a Hogarth curve design in two slender brass vases either side of the altar cross. Fortunately the dorsal in that church was just the right shade of red to make a background for the shocking-pink flowers, and their long golden stamens blended with the brass of the altar appointments.

Church flowers should be arranged reverently and without any thought of self-promotion.

Following is a list of flowers that are satisfactory for church arrangements.

FLOWERS SATISFACTORY FOR CHURCHES

Garden Flowers	Wildflowers	Florist's Flowers
Acacia	Black-eyed Susan	African Daisy
Aster	Boneset	Anemone
Astilbe	Daisy	Anthurium
Calendula	Goldenrod	Calla Lily
Canterbury Bell	Joe-Pye Weed	Camellia
Daffodil	Lily	Carnation
Dahlia	Queen Anne's Lace	Chrysanthemum
Day Lily	Viburnum	Easter Lily
Delphinium	Wild Aster	Freesia
Forsythia		Gladiolus
Foxglove		Heather
Chrysanthemum		Poinsettia
Hydrangea		Poker Plant
Iris		Rose
Lilac		Ranunculus
Lupine		Rubrum Lily
Marguerite		Shasta Daisy
Marigold		Snapdragon

Garden Flowers	*Florist's Flowers*
Mock Orange	Stock
Narcissus	Strelitzia
Peony	Tulip
Rhododendron	
Rose	
Thermopsis	
Tulip	
Veronica	
Vitex	

WEDDINGS

WEDDINGS are lucrative and legitimate business for florists, and for those who can afford their flowers and services there is no doubt that leaving the wedding decorations to them is an expedient solution. However, the expenses for a large wedding are so tremendous that many parents of brides who must watch their pennies find themselves involved with estimates and charges for unexpected items to the point where pleasure in the wedding is counteracted by worry over the bills.

To these people "a flower arranging friend" willing to help is a godsend. And as for the friend, what great joy to share in the happiest occasion of a young couple's life by doing something that gives her pleasure. I know that this is true because I have done it many times, and any help that it has been to the bride or her family cannot measure up to the joy that I have had myself.

For a very large church wedding, the amateur would be wise to confine her efforts to arrangements for the altar, with well-placed palms or ferns rented from a florist as a background. (Altar arrangements are described in Part V under "Church." But for the small church or home wedding, there are many ways to make the surroundings beautiful and individual. For one thing, once it is known that a friend is "doing" the flowers for a wedding, other friends and neighbors offer flowers from their yards and gardens, and you can take advantage of seasonal material like apple blossoms, rambler roses, lilacs, mock orange, white hydrangeas, and dogwood, which are a change from the usual carnations, snapdragons, gladiolus, and chrysanthemums.

I know of one elderly woman who grows unusually large and beautiful lilies of the valley by the thousands. The week her granddaughter was to be married, they were in full bloom. She invited a dozen or so of her young friends to a "morning coffee picking party." The younger women picked the flowers in bunches of fifty, while the older woman fed them delicious homemade coffee cake and coffee. Some of the blossoms were taken to the florist to be made into the bride's bouquet, and the rest the grandmother made into miniature bride's bouquets (using the Oasis holders described in Part I under "Mechanical Aids") for the center of the individual tables at the reception.

There is another woman, in a small Vermont town, who grows flowers in her garden primarily for the Sunday services in the little white church there, and for the wedding of any girl who is married there.

In a small church there are many ways to use flowers and greens to make it festive for a wedding. One that I had great joy in "doing" was a May wedding in a small Episcopal church at the seashore. It is a simple church, with varnished wooden walls and pews, a high vaulted ceiling and a lovely filigree brass chancel rail. The light is filtered through narrow stained-glass windows.

Instead of ferns or palms at the front of the church, we decided to use small natural seashore pine trees. A morning that I will always remember is the one when the bride's mother and I went into the spring woods to cut them. It had been raining, and the smell of the wet pine and moist spring earth mingled with the fresh smell of the sea was indescribable. We cut trees of various sizes, their new tips like pale green candles, piled them in a station wagon, and took them to the church, where we banked them either side of the altar, using heavy wire fastened to inconspicuous nails to hold them in place. The wedding was to be on Saturday, and we did this on the Wednesday before.

On Thursday we decorated the center aisle. We fastened standards, made by nailing a rectangular piece of plywood to a wooden pole, at every fifth pew. These were just a little taller than the end of the pew, and were varnished the same color as the wood in the church. We secured them with a broad elastic band. We fastened an aluminum freezer pan, sprayed dark green, to the plywood top with Stickum, fitted a soaked block of Oasis in it, and put a little water in the pan to keep the Oasis wet.

In this, we made perky bouquets of well-hardened white marguerites, green clusters of pachysandra and huckleberry. We covered the elastic bands with a loop of white ribbon, tying the ends in a bow on the aisle side. The effect was of an aisle of daisy clusters. (These looked as fresh when we dismantled them several days later, as they did then.) In the altar vases we made large arrangements of white lilacs and more marguerites. The whole effect was one of elegant simplicity. A plus that we didn't plan was the fragrance of the pine in the church the day of the wedding. It was so fresh that you could actually see people sniffing as they entered the church.

Another time the daughter of the minister of a sweet little white church in New England was to be married. Days before the wedding, women of the church gathered greens from the surrounding woods and made yards of roping. The day before the wedding they fastened this in garlands around the inside of the church. They also made bouquets of garden flowers and put them in water to harden. A couple of hours before the ceremony, they tied the bouquets to the ends of the pews with white ribbon. Again, I have never forgotten the fragrance as I entered that church or the exquisite simplicity of the decorations. Best of all, many people had a feeling of sharing in the ceremony.

When one of my friends, a widow, was to be married again in a chapel, she bought pots and pots of beautiful white chrysanthemums. Some of us arranged these, against a background of ferns, into a garden on the platform in front of the pulpit. There, surrounded by intimate friends, the couple was married. After the ceremony, each friend was given a pot of chrysanthemums as a remembrance.

The most peaceful time I had in the fun but hectic days preceding the wedding of one of my daughters was the quiet hour I spent in the church the morning of the wedding arranging the altar flowers. Although the main decorations were done by a florist, I reserved for myself that sentimental treat. There was more sentiment involved than just arranging them, too, for my mother had grown the flowers, handsome white Canterbury bells, from seed. At the ceremony the flower bells, swaying in the gentle breeze from an open window, seemed to be making a contribution to the music of the service.

Sometimes a flower arranging friend cannot take on the responsibility of the entire decorations of a church but would like to share her talent and garden flowers in some way. Arrangements of flowers on tables in the narthex or foyer of a church, or outside the front doors, are gracious and welcoming. I am thinking of a white Colonial church where tall green garden urns, filled with white peonies, flanked the opened outside doors. The flowers were grown by a neighbor of the bride and arranged by her. At another wedding, also in a white New England church, a friend cut seven-foot sprays of gorgeous crimson ramblers and arranged them in bronze umbrella stands at either side of the entrance.

A great help to a bride's mother would be for a flower arranging friend to be responsible for the bouquets on the small tables at a reception. These should be done in similar containers, and ones easy to use for such an occasion are the metal Oasis holders. These are inexpensive and readily available. However, at two weddings I made good use of coffee cans. These were painted white, then dabbled with silver. Crumpled chicken wire made the mechanics.

At the first wedding, on a typical June day, the tables were covered with pink cloths and the cans filled with crimson rambler roses, which just matched the velvet seats on the caterer's chairs. At the other wedding, on a hot July evening, when the bridesmaids wore pale green and carried bouquets of glossy dark green leaves centered with gardenias, the tables had pale green cloths. I made bouquets of mixed greens—laurel, andromeda, ilex, and yew—in the white containers, and put a tall white candle in the middle of each. They looked cool and different.

If you are doing tables for a reception, and only white table-cloths are available, get ribbon in whatever color is being used for the bridesmaids' dresses and cross it over the white cloths. Make arrangements of white flowers in Oasis holders and place them in the center of the table where the crossed ribbons meet.

Sometimes a flower arranging contribution can be as small as a nosegay for the top of a wedding cake. I know one woman who, learning that the tall stately bride was to carry calla lilies, made a miniature of her bouquet for the top of the wedding cake, using blossoms from her spathiphyllum houseplant, whose flowers look like miniature calla lilies.

WORKING WITH CHILDREN

ONE OF the most inspiring ways to share your flower arranging interest is to work with children. Children adore flower arranging, and have a natural talent. They are most original and completely uninhibited in the things they do. Their arrangements can be spiritual, humorous, beautiful, and sometimes macabre.

My first experience in working with them was organizing a flower show in an elementary school with two hundred and fifty pupils. The day of the show they made over six hundred exhibits. There are many things I remember vividly about that show: more boys won ribbons than girls, with the problem boy of the school winning three blues; there wasn't a pitcher or a teapot that didn't have flowers sticking from the spout; the incredulous look on the faces of adults as they looked at the show, and their spontaneous laughter as they recognized the humor in some of the exhibits; the exhibit by a kindergartner of a toy plastic washing machine foaming with lilies of the valley.

Three arrangements I remember particularly. Two were in a class "An Arrangement to Portray a Song Title." One was a scene with an open grave surrounded by flowers, with toy marching soldiers carrying a block for a coffin—the title, "Chopin's Funeral March." The other, in quite a different vein, was a charming bouquet of lilies of the valley and violets with one dead dandelion in the middle—the title "Stranger in Paradise." The third arrangement, done by an eight-year-old child in the class "An Arrangement to Portray a Book Title," was a naturalistic scene with a stump, moss, and ferns. Nestling against the stump was a narcissus bulb, and her title was "Sleeping Beauty." It was her own idea, and her mother was as surprised as anyone else at her subtlety.

Since that time I have worked with many children in many classes and flower shows, and they never cease to surprise me. Their enthusiasm, their lack of inhibition, and their direct approach are qualities that adults would do well to copy.

There are many ways for a flower arranger who is interested in children to share her talent with them, and what could possibly be more rewarding than to encourage a child in a hobby which may give him lifelong pleasure? One woman I know has a large cutting garden and lets neighborhood children pick flowers there and make arrangements under her guidance. Another did research with her Sunday School class on biblical plants, found some that would grow in the church garden, and made arrangements with them each Sunday for the altar in the Sunday School room. There are badges that Girl Scouts earn for flower identification, table setting, flower arranging, and allied subjects. A troop leader would be overjoyed to have a flower arranger offer to help with instruction for these.

Many people are surprised when they learn of the wonderful work volunteers interested in flower arranging are doing with handicapped children. Administrators in homes and hospitals for handicapped children cannot speak too highly of the therapeutic value of working with flowers for the small patients.

I know of one little boy in a home for cerebral palsied children who can now hold a spoon to feed himself because he became so interested in terrarium making under the guidance of a "flower lady" that one day he finally lifted a fistful of sand from a container to the terrarium bowl—the first time that he had successfully lifted an object from one place to another. That was the first step in lifting a spoon from a bowl to his mouth.

I know of children in a heart hospital to whom working with flowers has brought much joy. Volunteer women give instruction to ambulatory patients in planting flowers. (The heavy work is done for them.) As the flowers grow, they instruct the children in flower identification and the rudiments of flower arrangement. At the end of the summer they have a flower show, complete with judges. (One little girl was disappointed that they didn't wear long black robes.) After the judging the children took the arrangements to the ones who were bedridden.

Even children in homes for the blind work with flowers with the help of women volunteers. They learn to identify flowers by smell and feel. They have flower shows, where they are given identical papier-mâché containers and are allowed to choose their own flowers from the garden by touch. The entry cards and awards are written in Braille, and it is a touching sight to see children enter a room and feel the cards with their fingers, their faces lighting up when they realize they have won a ribbon.

Mentally retarded children are fascinated by simple instruction in flower arrangement. They can be given a lump of floral clay and some uncomplicated dried material and make an arrangement by following lines drawn on a blackboard. Their delight in the result is unequaled by any blue ribbon winner in a flower show.

Without exception people who have talked to me about their work in these projects with children have said that not only is it rewarding to them but that they are continually amazed at the interest and enthusiasm shown by the children.

GIFTS

FOR AN especially thoughtful gift, something associated with flowers is often the answer. Sometimes it is hard to find just the right thing to say thank you to a host or hostess. Perhaps you are tired of giving the usual things as wedding presents. Maybe you want to give something that is uniquely for a certain person.

Last fall, after a wonderful visit in Bermuda, I wanted to send something meaningful to my hosts. Nothing from a shop seemed just right. Suddenly one day I had an idea. I had collected pods and cones while I was there, and I decided to make a Christmas wreath using material from their house and ours. From their house were casuarina cones, false Indian almond, pods from Dutchman's-pipe, and rattail cones, and from ours, Japanese black pine cones, mallow pods, milkweed pods, lily pods, dock, and some fascinating clusters from our roadside that I still can't name. The card read, "Everything on the wreath grew within a hundred yards of your house or mine." I have never had a more enthusiastic thank you note.

I know of a flower arranger who, at the time of a wedding, finds out from the bride's mother where in her house she would like an arrangement. (Even if the wedding is not to be at home, there are always festivities connected with it and you want the house to look its best.) Then she selects a container that is suitable for the desired spot, makes an arrangement in it, and gives the container to the bride for a wedding present.

If your wedding present to a bride is one that can hold flowers, you can have an arrangement in it that will add decoration to the display of wedding gifts. You might fill a brass planter with white geraniums, or an antique glass spoonholder with a bunch of lilies of the valley. Another charming present that never fails to delight a bride is a pair of framed arrangements of dried or pressed flowers. It is fairly easy to find attractive old frames at auctions or in secondhand or antique shops. If you buy these when you see them, and restore them if necessary, and keep pressed and dried flowers on hand, you will never be at a loss for a present.

One woman, learning that a bride was to receive some white spray orchids from Hawaii as a present, offered to give as her present some of the glass bowls that fit in candlesticks and to arrange the orchids in them on the bridal table. I saw the table, and it was outstanding, with the orchids looking like delicate fountains.

Perhaps you have a friend who loved to walk in the woods but is no longer able to because of arthritis or other health reasons. In the spring why not make a little dish garden, using a shallow container, of tiny wild plants—wild geraniums, hepaticas, violets, and spring beauties? If you plant them when they are tiny, they will continue to grow and delight your friend for many days.

On May Day what could be a more appropriate way to show affection for a dear friend than to make a May basket like the one in Fig. 37?

A miniature arrangement is a happy choice for someone who is sick, for they can keep it by their bedside, and enjoy its minute beauty at close range.

A miniature arrangement proved the perfect gift for my youngest daughter to give her aunt one Christmas. My sister collects authentic miniature furniture, which she has in shadow-box rooms, everything in perfect scale, including wallpaper, rugs, and accessories. My daughter found a discarded individual silver salt shaker and, using the top as a container, she made a miniature arrangement for the dining room table in the miniature dining room. She used tiny pieces of dried material like statice, artemisia tips, and minute bits of cockscomb. The holes in the shaker top held the dried material, and the result looked like a typical eighteenth-century mass arrangement in a silver bowl, perfectly suited to the miniature dining room. It was her aunt's favorite present.

An amusing gift for someone would be a hat made of real flowers. It could be for Easter, for a garden club speaker or presi-

Arrangement by Myra Brooks

Figure 37. A straw hat forms a basket for a May Day arrangement of forsythia, tulips, daisies, daffodils, and hyacinths. (Photo by Roche)

dent, or to wear to a wedding. You can buy velvet-covered wire frames at a five-and-ten or a variety store. Wire the flowers as you would for a corsage, and cover them with green florist's tape. You can twist them around the frame wherever you want them. Flowers suitable to use would be carnations, roses, day lilies, chrysanthemums, camellias, and gardenias.

Gather autumn leaves in the fall, press them, and keep them for gift packages. Boxes wrapped in white, yellow, green, orange, or red glazed paper or foil are stunning with autumn leaves scattered on top. Glue them to the paper with rubber cement.

An enchanting gift for someone who loves a garden, and which is reminiscent of our grandmothers' linen cupboards, is a jar of potpourri. This is made from a combination of flower petals and spices, whose scent can fill a room, a closet, or a bureau drawer.

To make potpourri, gather flower petals from your garden that are just at the peak of their bloom. Since you want them to dry quickly, pick them when it hasn't rained for twenty-four hours and when they are not covered with dew. Because you want them for fragrance, gather sweet-smelling flowers like mock orange, violets, heliotrope, verbena, pinks, and daphne. Rose petals should predominate, so gather lots of rose petals, and remember that some of the old-fashioned ones like moss rose or cabbage rose are the most fragrant.

There are several ways of drying the petals. You can spread them on absorbent paper towels on a flat surface in an airy room, or put them on a wire screen or hardware cloth so that the air can circulate around them. Or, you can spread them out in the sun in a sheltered spot.

Whatever method you use, when they are perfectly dry, they are ready to be mixed with other ingredients. To four quarts of rose petals add a handful of petals from other fragrant flowers, and a half handful each of the minced leaves of three or four herbs like mint, rosemary, thyme, bay leaf, laurel, or marjoram. There are many old and favorite recipes for adding spices and oils. Here is one. Mix together

> 1 lb. table salt
> ½ oz. storax
> 1 oz. oil of bergamot
> ½ oz. orrisroot
> ½ teaspoon allspice
> 1 oz. powdered clove

Put the flowers and the spice mixture in alternate layers in a crock, stir them well, and cover tightly. When the mixture is well blended, put it into other small covered containers—small apothecary jars, empty bath salts bottles, spice bottles, or any others that are suitable.

INDEX

Page numbers printed in italics indicate illustrations.